RULE THE GAME

encompass
EDITIONS

Rule the Game: How Authority Marketing Leads the Pack
ISBN: 978-1-927664-21-6

© 2024 CJSM Publishing Inc. and A.S. Lycka
Library and Archives Canada Cataloguing in Publication
Lycka, Allen. S., 1956-

Published 2024 by Encompass Editions, Kingston, Ontario, Canada

Printed and bound in the U.S.A.

RULE
THE
GAME

How Authority Marketing Leads the Pack

Dr. Allen Steven Lycka

encompass
EDITIONS

CONTENTS

INTRODUCTION

WHY THIS BOOK

I wrote this book originally for the International Order of Fantastic Professionals (IOFP), an organization dedicated to helping professionals retain their elite status within their chosen area of expertise. I presented my paper on the subject in 2019 at Harvard. During the pandemic closures, many IOFP members' asked me to make it more specific to individuals who *aspire* to becoming experts. The evidence suggests that many — perhaps most — experts are unsure of the path they can follow to career success. That's the path I'll lay out for you here.

A shortcut to being recognized as an expert in your field is simply to join the IOFP. And a shortcut to that shortcut is to book a session with an IOFP concierge. They're there to help.

The IOFP brings together professionals from a wide spectrum of industries. As a member, you'll communicate and collaborate 24/7 with other members in the organization's private LinkedIn chatroom. In the process you'll gain greater recognition, access online support, and meet top-tier professionals including the author of this book, the FAMOUS Dr. AL.

When you join the IOFP, follow the 13-step formula I teach (especially the Triangle of Pre-eminence™), and adopt the strategies put forward in these books, you'll stand on the shoulders of giants to achieve just as they've achieved.

Members of the IOFP are chosen through a rigorous selection process that identifies them as the *crème de la crème* of professionals in their professions and industries. Candidates prove they have "the right stuff" and as an emblem of their achievement, those successfully admitted receive a one-of-a-kind award and certificate attesting to their abilities. They are featured on over 200 unique news services, including CNN, ABC, FOX, Telemundo and CW and attend a gala dinner to celebrate their achievement.

Looking back at my journey over half a century as a leading cosmetic doctor, celebrity, professional speaker, mentor, author, syndicated radio show producer, and host, I know I could have gone much further with far less effort if I'd allowed others to help me. That's why I'm helping you by sharing secrets that will accelerate your climb to the pinnacle of expert status.

The easiest path to success is to be acknowledged as the expert in your field, then collaborating and interacting with other experts. When you stand on the shoulders of those who've gone before, the path is suddenly easier to see, and that path can become a money-making machine.

I outlined many of these concepts in a speech I gave in 2019 at Harvard University called "What They Didn't Teach You in Business School". During the two years that followed, the COVID pandemic shut everything down, but this allowed my ideas to crystalize and the IOFP was born.

There is an old African saying that "If you want to go fast, go alone. But if you want to go far, go together." Come together with us on this journey.

WHO I AM AND WHY YOU SHOULD LISTEN TO ME

Many so-called gurus claim to have all the answers but as we learn, many do not hold up to scrutiny. Please subject me to that same scrutiny.

Certainly I've travelled an unconventional path to business success.

Here are some highlights:

- BSC Honors Psychology University of Calgary in Calgary, Alberta, Canada
- Graduated 1983 University of Alberta MD
- Interned Misericordia Hospital, Edmonton, AB, Canada 1983-84
- Completed two years Internal Medicine U of 1984-86
- Completed Residency in Dermatology University of Minnesota 1986-89
- 16 CONSECUTIVE CONSUMER CHOICE AWARDS FOR BEST IN COSMETIC SURGERY
- 2013 Philanthropist of the Year
- Over 20,000 Patients seen
- Over 27,000 procedures performed

Currently, I'm the host and executive producer of the syndicated radio show *Live with the Famous Dr. Al* (formerly *How to Live a Fantastic Life*) with over 7 million listeners a six times bLU talk speaker, two times TEDx speaker, and three times an Internationally acclaimed bestselling author. I am the Doctor of Positivity and Happiness.

Here are some speeches I've given:

- Harvard University - Oct 2019
- UCLA - 2023
- TEDx Grande Prairie -2020

- TEDx U of A 2024
- University of Calgary July 2023
- University of Alberta August 2022, 2023
- Anderson University Oct 2023
- Disrupt HR Las Vegas Sept 2023
- Disrupt HR Northern Colorado Oct 2023
- Disrupt HR Waterloo- Kitchner Oct 2023
- Disrupt HR San Antonio, Oct 2023
- Disrupt Greenville, SC - Nov 2023
- Disrupt HR - Sioux Falls April 2024
- Disrupt HR Albuquerque April 2024
- Disrupt Austin May 2024
- Disrupt Los Angeles May 2024
- Disrupt Chicago May 2024
- Disrupt Halifax May 2024
- Disrupt Portland, ME, June 2024
- PBS event — May 2024
- SHRM Sandusky, Ohio September 2024
- SHRM Grand Forks, N.D Sept 2024
- SHRM Tennessee August 2024
- SHRM Albuquerque - April 2024
- ProEd CMED's - Phoenix November 2024
- NFDA New Orleans - Oct 2024
- Tony Walker Financial - Bowling Green Kentucky, Oct 2024
- WFLA Spokane May 2024
- IAOTP Toronto July 2024
- Iowa Hospital Association Nov 2023
- National Management Week Sept 2023

- DASIL Ho ChiMinh City, 2017
- DASIL Sun City, South Africa 2017
- CSF - Las Vegas, Nashville December 2015-2018
- CSI- Dubai 2016
- AAD - Multiple cities -2003-2017
- CSF - Las Vegas 2003 - 2018
- CSF - Nashville- 2018

There are a few things I can claim

- The #1 Authority in Authority Marketing
- The #1 Expert in Overcoming Obstacles. In Life
- The #1 Expert in Living A Fantastic Life
- The Doctor of Positivity and Happiness
- International best-selling co-author with Harriet Tinka
- "Secrets of Living a Fantastic Life"
- International best-selling co-author with Jack Canfield -The Pillars of Success
- International best-selling co-author with Corey Porier BLU Vol 1 - Business, Life and the Universe Volume 1
- Host and Executive Director of Live with the FAMOUS Dr AL with over 7 million listeners a month
- CEO and President of IOFP (I
- International Order of Fantastic Professionals
- Philanthropist of the year- Edmonton - 2003
- #1 speaker, mentor and author for 2024 by the IAOTP. (International Association of Top Professionals)

In summary, I know a thing or two about a thing or two and I want to share them with you. Together we'll shorten your path to the summit of authority in your field.

THE SCHOOL OF HARD KNOCKS: LIFE'S ULTIMATE BUSINESS CLASSROOM

In the vast arena of business education, traditional pathways like MBAs and prestigious internships are often highlighted as golden tickets to success. However, there exists a more unconventional and grueling educator that has sculpted many of the world's most successful entrepreneurs: the school of hard knocks. This metaphorical institution doesn't boast lush campuses or gleaming trophies; it offers real-life experiences, failures, and the relentless reality of trial and error as its core curriculum.

The school of hard knocks teaches its lessons through the unforgiving reality of business battles. Unlike classroom settings where mistakes are theoretical, real-world business mistakes carry significant consequences, thus offering essential and concrete lessons. Each setback and failure is a unique opportunity to learn something that cannot be taught in the serene environment of a classroom. This tenacious educator instills knowledge and cultivates adaptability, a critical quality in the constantly changing business environment.

Steve Jobs, co-founder of Apple Inc., famously dropped out of college and endured numerous career lows—including being ousted from the very company he started. These harsh lessons from the school of hard knocks didn't just educate him; they forged his revolutionary approach to business and technology. Job's business journey is a testament to the idea that real-world experiences can provide a depth of knowledge and resilience that traditional education often fails to impart. Another graduate from this school is Oprah Winfrey, who overcame a tumultuous upbringing and multiple career setbacks before becoming a media mogul. Through her experiences, she gained invaluable business skills such as perseverance, adaptability, and a deep understanding of human emotions. These skills played a crucial role in her journey of building a successful broadcasting and media empire.

The school of hard knocks curriculum is immensely diverse, tailored by personal experiences and the specific challenges one faces. For instance, it teaches risk management through actual financial stakes, such as investing in a failed startup. It provides insights into human resource management by exploring real-life interpersonal conflicts and their resolutions, such as effectively leading a team with diverse personalities. Additionally, it provides insights into customer behavior through direct interactions and feedback, such as dealing with customer complaints or understanding market demand.

Moreover, this school instills an entrepreneurial spirit driven by necessity rather than a purely theoretical desire to innovate. This spirit is evident in individuals who establish businesses due to the necessity of survival and success, drawing upon their personal experiences with unmet market demands and neglected customer requirements.

Critically, the school of hard knocks imparts a unique wisdom about failure. In traditional business education, failure is often stigmatized, something to be avoided at all costs. However, in the real world, failure is a nuanced teacher. It shows us what doesn't work and toughens our psychological and emotional resilience. The ability to bounce back from failure, learn from it, and progress is an invaluable lesson that fosters self-assurance in our capacity to surmount obstacles.

Networking, a critical element of business success, is also learned on this battleground. The relationships that are established through mutual support and shared struggles frequently endure for an entire lifetime. They are typically more practical and profound than those developed in business schools' calm, competitive environment.

Of course, the school of hard knocks is not without its risks. The costs of failure here can be high, potentially leading to financial ruin, mental health struggles, and personal turmoil. Therefore, while the lessons learned are invaluable, they come with high stakes. This necessitates a balanced approach to learning, combining real-world experience with formal education when possible to mitigate risks and maximize learning. This comprehension provides us with a comprehensive knowledge base, guaranteeing that we are adequately prepared for the forthcoming obstacles.

In conclusion, while traditional education certainly has its place in business learning, the school of hard knocks offers profound lessons rooted in reality. It educates through experience, resilience, and reality, producing graduates who are well-equipped to navigate the complexities of the business world. For many successful entrepreneurs, the most formidable challenges and setbacks have been their most instructive experiences, proving that sometimes, life's hardest lessons are its most valuable.

Let me ask you a question: do you really want the school of hard knocks as your teacher? Where are you covered in blood, toil, tears and sweat? And you recall each glove that strikes you, causing you to collapse and scream in agony? I suggest you take this easier road. Stand on the "shoulders of giants." The air is clearer; the view helps you see all obstacles in your way. That's the way of the IOFP - the International Order of Fantastic Professionals.

TEACHERS

You must have tremendous teachers to be a leading cosmetic surgeon and businessman with all the accolades I have received. Many teachers have taught me valuable lessons. I will share them with you.

DAN S. KENNEDY

Dan S. Kennedy, a master of direct marketing, entrepreneurship and business strategy, is an acclaimed author, speaker, and marketing consultant His teachings have empowered countless entrepreneurs and businesses to achieve peak performance and maximize their marketing efficacy. Let us delve into the essence of Kennedy's philosophy by examining ten core principles that encapsulate his teachings as one of the world's leading business educators.

I stumbled across Dan when I picked up a book at the local Staples office supply store. I was immediately attracted to his no B.S. style. At the end of his book, he made a no-obligation offer to readers that they send in their material, and he would critique it for free. I did this.

Six weeks later, he mailed me a reply. With that reply was an offer to attend a "mastermind meeting" in Akron, Ohio. There began a decade of Dan Kennedy as my mentor. I was featured in many of his early no b.s. Books. Here's a letter of recommendation Dan wrote about me:

> "I have been asked to write a testimonial for my old friend and student, Dr. Allen Lycka. As both of us realize, as we get older, these ties that bind are even more important because our days are limited. I've known him for over 3 decades. He came to me fresh out of dermatology school and was bright-eyed and bushy tailed. But he distinguished himself as one of the greatest cosmetic doctors of

all time despite being told in 2003 that he had ALS (Lou Gehrig's disease) and that he better get his affairs in order because he only had 6 months to live. Blind persistence and determination pulled him through, and I have covered him in over a half dozen of my books and in 2 books I co-authored with him. I even co-owned a racehorse with him, and I remember him saying he wanted the pooing end cause it costs less".

"My friend Dr Lycka has shared with me that he left his profession of medicine, but unlike Elvis, he did not leave the building. He has joined the world's second oldest profession - a speaker, a coach, and an author. He writes under his nom de plume, Dr. Allen Lycka because he was so typecast and famous as a surgeon that his followers couldn't believe he could do anything else. They laughed when he said he'd write a bestseller in the Great Pandemic of 2020 but not when it became a bestseller based on pre-sales alone. Because he didn't stop there – he wrote 5 more, one in conjunction with #1 New York Times best seller Jack Canfield called "Pillars of Success". His current book, "Authority," is a classic and should be on everyone's shelf. Do yourself a favor- buy his books, hire him as a keynote speaker, seek him out as a coach, and listen to his podcasts. Get every bit of wisdom you can from him while you still can".

Dan S. Kennedy, Author of bestselling NO BS business series including NO BS Guide To Marketing to the Affluent, and of Almost Alchemy, More From Fewer & Less; Multi-Decade Strategic Advisor & Coach to Professional Practices, Serial Entrepreneur

Now - enough about me and more about Dan Kennedy. Here are some of the things he taught me:

1. **The Power of Direct Marketing:** Kennedy champions the power of direct marketing to reach out to customers personally, persuasively, and profitably. Unlike traditional advertising, direct marketing is all about measurable responses. He teaches

businesses to focus on targeted communications and trackable results, ensuring that every marketing dollar spent is an investment with a quantifiable return.

2. **Understanding the Market's Psychology:** A central tenet of Kennedy's teachings is the importance of understanding customer psychology. He believes successful marketing speaks directly to customers' desires, fears, and needs. Kennedy's strategies often involve crafting messages that resonate emotionally, encouraging customers to act based not just on logic but emotion.

3. **The Importance of Unique Value Propositions:** Kennedy stresses the importance of differentiating one's business with a Unique Selling Proposition (USP). He teaches that a strong USP gives customers clear reasons to choose your business over competitors. According to Kennedy, this differentiation should be obvious and compelling, rooted in the real benefits that the customer will enjoy.

4. **Leveraging Higher Prices:** Unlike many business advisors who focus on competitive pricing, Kennedy often advocates for premium pricing strategies. He argues that businesses can charge more by adding value through superior service, quality, or perceived exclusivity. Higher prices not only increase margins but also position a brand as a high-value leader in its market.

5. **Strategic Copywriting:** Kennedy is a master copywriter and asserts that persuasive writing is at the heart of effective marketing. He imparts specific strategies for crafting persuasive copy that encourages readers to purchase or perform a desired action, emphasizing the significance of compelling narratives, headlines, and calls to action.

6. **Creating Magnetic Offers:** One of Kennedy's key strategies is the creation of irresistible offers. An offer, he suggests, should be so enticing that the target customer feels compelled to act immediately. This involves a combination of value, relevance,

and urgency. Kennedy teaches that a well-crafted offer often includes bonuses, guarantees, and limited-time promotions to increase its appeal.

7. **Time Management for Entrepreneurs:** Kennedy doesn't just teach marketing; he also focuses on productivity and time management for entrepreneurs. He preaches disciplined time management, prioritizing activities directly contributing to revenue generation. His methods help entrepreneurs avoid common pitfalls like over-scheduling and multitasking, which can dilute focus and effectiveness.

8. **The Role of Personality in Business:** Kennedy believes in the power of personal branding and personality in business. He teaches that customers buy from people they like, trust, and find interesting. Kennedy's approach involves integrating the entrepreneur's personality into the brand, making customer interactions more relatable and engaging.

9. **Systems and Scalability:** A crucial aspect of Kennedy's teachings is the creation of systems that allow for scalability. He emphasizes that for a business to grow, it must have repeatable, scalable systems in place. This includes everything from marketing funnels and sales processes to customer service protocols and backend operations.

10. **Continuous Learning and Adaptation:** Finally, Kennedy advocates for ongoing education and adaptation in business. He argues that staying informed and flexible is key to sustained success in the ever-evolving landscape of marketing and entrepreneurship. He encourages business leaders to continually test new strategies, learn from the results, and refine their approaches accordingly.

In conclusion, Dan S. Kennedy's business teaching approach is strategic and practical. His lessons are actionable and can be immediately implemented to achieve tangible results, transcending basic business theories. Kennedy's enduring influence is a testament to the effectiveness of his methods and the timeless nature of his teachings. By embracing these principles, entrepreneurs can survive and thrive in the competitive business world.

Solving Problems the Dan S. Kennedy Way: No-Nonsense Strategies for Business Success

When you're in the thick of business warfare, problems are akin to landmines that await an unwary step. Navigating through them requires a tested, battle-hardened strategy rather than just any approach. Dan S. Kennedy, with his no-nonsense, straightforward style, has always advocated for facing problems head-on, armed with an arsenal of direct-response marketing tactics and a hardened entrepreneurial mindset.

1. **Identify the Real Problem, Not Just the Symptoms**

   The first step in Kennedy-esque problem-solving is to drill down to the root cause. Businesses often mistake symptoms for the problem itself. For instance, if sales are plummeting, the immediate reaction might be to change the sales team. However, the real issue could be outdated products, poor customer service, or even ineffective marketing messages. Kennedy's approach would be to take a step back, analyze the entire system, and identify the real culprits responsible for the symptoms.

2. **Cut Through the Fluff**

   Kennedy's mantra is to cut through the fluff. This means making decisions quickly and decisively without being bogged down by unnecessary details or over-analysis. In the business world, time is money, and every moment spent in indecision is a missed opportunity. Clarity and directness save time and yield results, regardless of whether you're crafting a marketing message or deciding on a new product launch.

3. **Leverage Direct Response Marketing**

   One of Kennedy's core solutions to many business problems is the use of direct response marketing. This solution is not solely about making sales; it's about creating a measurable response from every ad, every mailing, and every campaign. When facing a problem like declining customer engagement, Kennedy would likely implement a targeted campaign that directly addresses the customer's needs, tracks the responses, and adjusts in real-time to optimize results.

4. **Use Strategic Thinking, Not Just Tactical Reactions**

   In problem-solving, Kennedy underscores the significance of strategic over tactical thinking. Tactical reactions are about short-term solutions, which might seem to solve a problem but often only serve as a temporary fix. Strategic thinking, however, involves looking at the bigger picture and planning for long-term success. For example, if a business struggles with cash flow issues, Kennedy would advise revising pricing strategies, modifying payment terms, or reevaluating the entire business model for sustainability rather than just finding immediate financial injections.

5. **Implement Robust Testing and Tracking**

   Kennedy has always been a proponent of rigorous testing and tracking. Any solution to a problem should be tested on a small scale before full implementation. This allows you to see real-world results and make necessary adjustments without risking too much capital or resources. Whether it's a new marketing campaign, a product feature, or a customer service enhancement, testing and tracking provide the data needed to make informed decisions.

6. **Focus on High-Return Activities**

   Kennedy would often point out that not all business activities are created equal. To solve problems effectively, focus on activities that offer the highest return on investment. This could entail prioritizing marketing efforts that directly result in sales or streamlining operations to reduce costs. It's about leveraging your resources in areas where they can make the biggest impact rather than spreading them too thinly across multiple fronts.

7. **Demand Accountability**

In any business environment, accountability is key. When problems arise, it's essential to have clear lines of responsibility. This not only ensures that issues are addressed promptly but also helps prevent them in the future. Kennedy would advocate for a culture where everyone from the top down knows their role in solving problems and is held accountable for their part of the process.

8. **Keep Your Customers at the Center**

Finally, Kennedy's approach to problem-solving always brings the focus back to the customer. Every solution should ultimately enhance the customer's experience or solve a problem for them. The end goal is to meet and exceed customer expectations, thereby driving loyalty and revenue, whether adjusting product offerings, improving service, or refining marketing messages,

§

In conclusion, Dan S. Kennedy's approach to solving business problems is grounded in practicality, strategic thinking, and a sharp focus on results. By adopting these no-nonsense strategies, businesses can navigate their challenges more effectively and position themselves for long-term success. Remember, in Kennedy's words, "In the real world of business, it's not the big that eat the small; it's the fast that eat the slow."

BRENDON BURCHARD

After the decade with Dan, I sought to broaden my horizons. I heard about Brendon Burchard, an up-and-coming powerhouse. I joined his mastermind group.

Brendon Burchard is a pivotal figure in personal development and business strategy. Recognized globally for his expertise in teaching high performance and personal growth, Burchard has empowered a generation of entrepreneurs and business professionals with tools to achieve sustained high performance in both their personal and professional lives.

Here are ten core principles that were instilled in me by Brendon Burchard, presented in a way that reflects the teaching style of the world's top business instructor. These principles are theoretical concepts and practical tools that empower individuals to achieve sustained high performance in their personal and professional lives.

1. **Seek Clarity:** Burchard emphasizes the importance of clarity to high performance. He encourages individuals to continuously seek clarity in four significant areas: self, social, skills, and service. By understanding who you want to be, how you want to interact with others, what skills you need to develop to succeed, and how you want to serve others, you can make more deliberate choices and align your actions with your true intentions.

2. **Generate Energy:** According to Burchard, maintaining high performance requires active energy generation and conservation. This includes managing physical energy through health and fitness and mental energy through practices like meditation and mindfulness. The aim is to sustain the vigor and stamina needed to tackle challenges and excel in one's endeavors.

3. **Raise Necessity:** High performers operate with a sense of necessity. This involves developing a compelling reason to perform well, often rooted in a deep understanding of identity or obligation to others. Burchard emphasizes the importance of believing in the necessity of our efforts, as it enhances our focus and determination.

4. **Increase Productivity:** Burchard stresses the importance of output in determining success in any field. He teaches specific strategies for managing time effectively, emphasizing the need to focus on what he calls "prolific quality output" in the areas that matter most. This involves prioritization, delegation, and saying no to tasks that do not align with key goals.

5. **Develop Influence:** Successful people develop influence in their fields. Burchard teaches how to build trust and respect through consistent value creation, empathetic communication, and leading by example. According to Burchard, influence helps people garner the support and resources needed to achieve great things.

6. **Demonstrate Courage:** It is crucial to consistently express your beliefs, share your ideas, take bold actions, and stand up for yourself and others, even in the face of fear, uncertainty, or potential conflict. Burchard believes that courage is a fundamental trait that drives personal and professional success.

7. **Practice Gratitude and Positive Thinking:** Burchard emphasizes the power of a positive mindset, which includes being grateful for your current circumstances and optimistic about future possibilities. This outlook fosters resilience, creativity, and an openness to opportunities.

8. **Envision a Long-term Future:** Burchard encourages people to think long-term and consider the legacy they want to leave. This long-range thinking helps individuals to stay motivated and focused, even when faced with short-term obstacles.

9. **Build Strong Habits:** Success is not a result of occasional acts of heroism but the product of daily habits. Burchard advises creating and sustaining habits that support your goals and improve your overall effectiveness and well-being.

10. **Cultivate a Support Network:** No one achieves greatness in isolation. Burchard emphasizes the significance of establishing and maintaining a network of mentors, supporters, and colleagues who can provide advice, feedback, and encouragement. A strong support network accelerates professional growth and offers critical emotional and social resources.

§

Brendon Burchard's teachings blend deep insights into the psychology of achievement with practical advice on how to apply these insights in real-world scenarios. His inspirational and systematic approach blueprints personal excellence and business success. Through his books, online courses, and seminars, Burchard has crafted a comprehensive system for achieving sustained high performance, making him a revered figure among modern business teachers. His influence continues to shape the strategies of ambitious individuals and organizations aiming for peak performance and exceptional results.

TONY ROBBINS

Tony Robbins, a name synonymous with peak performance and transformational leadership, has firmly established himself as one of the great business teachers of our time. His dynamic personal and professional development approach has influenced millions, from aspiring entrepreneurs to seasoned executives. As we delve into Robbins's philosophy and teachings, it becomes evident why he is revered as a luminary in the business world.

I met Tony at a day-long Edmonton workshop in January 2018. He profoundly impacted me because one of the first books I read in the self-help area was his book "The Giant Within". Here are ten core principles that Tony Robbins teaches, each a cornerstone of his approach to business and personal success:

1. **The Power of State Management:** Robbins emphasizes managing one's emotional and mental state. He believes that the state we operate in dictates our actions and results. Techniques such as physiology changes, focused breathing, and positive mental framing are essential for maintaining a peak state, enabling individuals to perform at their best under any circumstances.

2. **Setting Clear Goals:** According to Robbins, clarity is power. He advocates setting specific, measurable, achievable, relevant, and time-bound (SMART) goals. Robbins encourages people to dream big and clearly define what they want to achieve,

breaking down significant goals into actionable steps that lead to massive success.

3. **The Science of Achievement and the Art of Fulfillment:** Robbins teaches that success is about achieving goals and leading a fulfilling life. He distinguishes between the science of achievement, which can be systematized and replicated, and the art of fulfillment, which is personal and unique to each individual—balancing these two leads to success and true happiness.

4. **Taking Massive Action:** One of Robbins' most famous teachings is taking massive action. He posits that just having knowledge is not enough; it must be applied. Decisive and bold action is what differentiates successful people from the rest. This action must be persistent and adaptive to overcome the inevitable challenges that arise.

5. **Embracing the Power of Beliefs:** Robbins often discusses the power of beliefs in shaping our actions and, by extension, our realities. He encourages individuals to recognize and revise limiting beliefs that impede success, replacing them with empowering beliefs that advance them.

6. **Mastering the Art of Communication:** Effective communication is pivotal in Robbins' teaching. He asserts that how we communicate with others and ourselves ultimately determines the quality of our lives. Mastery of verbal and non-verbal communication enables individuals to influence others and create better relationships.

7. **Financial Intelligence:** Robbins dedicates much of his teaching to financial education. He stresses the importance of creating multiple income streams, investing wisely, and saving for the future. Understanding money management and financial markets empowers individuals to grow and protect their wealth.

8. **Continuous Learning and Growth:** Tony Robbins is a staunch advocate for lifelong learning. He believes constant personal and professional improvement is essential to staying relevant and successful. This involves reading extensively, attending workshops, and seeking mentorship.

9. **Leveraging the Power of Proximity:** Robbins suggests that "proximity is power." He advises surrounding oneself with mentors, peers, and teams who inspire and challenge you to grow. The networks and relationships we cultivate provide opportunities, advice, and support to advance our endeavors.

10. **Contributing Beyond Oneself:** Robbins teaches that true fulfillment comes from serving others. The more we give, the more we stand to receive—not just materially but spiritually and emotionally. This principle of contribution ensures a sense of purpose and deep satisfaction in one's personal and professional life.

§

Tony Robbins' teachings blend motivational practices with practical strategies, making his advice inspirational and highly actionable. His holistic approach ensures that individuals are equipped to succeed in business and all aspects of life. His influence continues to grow as he teaches, guides, and mentors the current and next generation of business leaders. Through his books, seminars, and coaching, Robbins has become a beacon of knowledge, empowerment, and transformation in the global business landscape, genuinely embodying the voice of the world's best business teacher.

WARREN BUFFETT

Warren Buffett, the Oracle of Omaha, has long been a beacon of investment wisdom and financial sagacity. His philosophy, grounded in the practical principles of value investing and prudence, has shaped his career and influenced countless others in finance and beyond. Herein, we delve into ten practical and fundamental principles taught by Buffett, which encapsulate his approach to investing and business management.

Warren and his teachings have deeply influenced my school of thoughts. I have attended 2 Berkshire Hathaway shareowner meetings, and I've written everything written by and about Buffet:

1. **The Principle of Value Investing:** Warren Buffett's cornerstone investment strategy is value investing, a concept pioneered by his mentor, Benjamin Graham. This principle advocates investing in companies whose shares appear underpriced relative to their intrinsic value. Buffett's acumen lies in distinguishing these diamonds in the rough, companies with solid fundamentals but temporarily undervalued by the market. His approach requires rigorous analysis and a deep understanding of the business, ensuring that investments are cheap and fundamentally sound.

2. **A Long-Term Perspective:** Buffett famously stated, "Our favorite holding period is forever." This highlights his belief in the long-term approach, eschewing the frenetic trading that

characterizes much of Wall Street's activities. For Buffett, patience is not merely a virtue but a potent strategic element of successful investing. By focusing on the long-term potential of investments, he avoids the pitfalls of short-term market fluctuations, which are often driven by sentiment rather than substance. This enduring approach can lead to substantial wealth creation over time.

3. **Investing in Quality Businesses:** Quality, for Buffett, is synonymous with companies possessing a 'moat'—a unique competitive advantage that allows them to fend off competitors and maintain profitability. This could be a strong brand, proprietary technology, or regulatory barriers. Investing in such companies ensures the business can sustain its competitive edge and generate value for shareholders over time.

4. **Financial Prudence:** Buffett's approach to finance is marked by a conservative management of debt and a strong emphasis on liquidity. He advocates maintaining robust cash reserves to seize opportunities as they arise, particularly during market downturns when others are constrained by financial stress. This prudence ensures Buffett's investments survive and thrive, regardless of economic conditions.

5. **Risk Management:** "Risk comes from not knowing what you're doing," Buffett remarks, encapsulating his approach to risk. He insists on investing within his 'circle of competence,' understanding the ins and outs of the business sectors where he deploys capital. This knowledge is critical in assessing the real risks associated with any investment, allowing him to avoid ventures where the outcomes are uncertain or beyond his control.

6. **Think Like an Owner:** Buffett's philosophy entails thinking like an owner rather than a mere shareholder. This perspective drives him to focus on the long-term health of the company, its market position, and operational stability. By adopting an

owner's mindset, investors are more likely to commit to companies that believe in the fundamental business model and management.

7. **Harnessing Market Fluctuations:** Buffett uses market volatility to his advantage instead of fearing it. He views significant market dips as buying opportunities, often quoting that it's wise to be "fearful when others are greedy, and greedy when others are fearful." His success has come not from timing the market but from capitalizing on the fear and irrationality of other investors.

8. **The Virtue of Simplicity:** Buffett avoids businesses whose models are challenging to understand. This principle ensures that investments are made in areas with clear potential risks and returns. This simplicity enables more accurate assessments of future performance and guards against the dangers inherent in opaque or overly complex ventures.

9. **Integrity and Trustworthiness:** For Buffett, the character of the management is as vital as the company's financial metrics. He invests in leaders who demonstrate integrity and honesty, believing that the trustworthiness of those at the helm is critical to the long-term success of any business. This approach mitigates risks and aligns his investments with his ethical standards.

10. **Patience and Discipline:** Buffett teaches the importance of patience and discipline in investing. Sticking to a well-thought-out investment strategy differentiates a successful investor from the rest despite market pressures and tempting short-term gains. Buffett's disciplined approach, focusing on long-term gains rather than short-lived victories, has been a key to his enduring success.

11. **Education:** Often your best investment is in yourself and your education

§

In conclusion, Warren Buffett's investment principles transcend the specifics of market trends or economic cycles. They are a blueprint for thoughtful, principled investing based on a deep understanding of business fundamentals, ethical leadership, and a commitment to long-term value creation. These principles have not only shaped Buffett's career but have also led to his enduring success, offering invaluable lessons for investors and managers alike. They emphasize a disciplined, informed, and ethical approach to business and investment, instilling confidence in their effectiveness.

BILL GATES

In business education, few figures are as compelling and instructive as Bill Gates. Gates, widely recognized as the world's foremost business educator, employs a combination of actionable teaching, insightful strategy, and relentless innovation that is well-received by both young entrepreneurs and seasoned executives. He has carved out a niche for himself by mastering the art of business and effectively imparting this wisdom to others. Here, I will explore why Bill Gates is celebrated as a superb business teacher and outline ten essential teachings he advocates, collectively forming a blueprint for business success.

Why Bill Gates is a Celebrated Business Teacher

1. **Real-World Experience:** Bill Gates's teachings are grounded in extensive real-world business experience. Having navigated the ups and downs of numerous ventures, his lessons are not merely theoretical but tested in the crucible of enterprise. This real-world applicability makes his teachings immensely valuable.

2. **Empirical Approach:** He relies heavily on data-driven decision-making, teaching his students and followers to base their strategies on empirical evidence rather than gut feelings. This approach reduces risk and enhances the potential for success in highly competitive markets.

3. **Innovative Mindset:** Innovation is at the core of Gates's philosophy. He teaches that staying ahead of technological advancements and market trends is crucial. His ability to forecast industry shifts and translate these insights into teachable content is unmatched.

4. **Ethics and Responsibility:** Gates does not shy away from the ethical dimensions of business. He emphasizes the importance of building companies that seek profit and contribute positively to society. This holistic view is essential for sustainable success.

5. **Global Perspective:** Understanding globalization's impacts is another pillar of Gates's teachings. He prepares his students to operate in a globalized business environment, emphasizing cultural sensitivity and international market dynamics.

6. **Focus on Leadership Development:** Leadership is another central theme. Gates believes nurturing compelling, inspiring, ethical leaders is key to organizational success. His teachings often focus on developing leadership qualities among his students.

7. **Adaptability:** One of Gates's fundamental tenets is adaptability. In his view, pivoting and adapting to changing circumstances is a critical skill for any business leader. He teaches strategies for resilience and flexibility in business planning and execution.

8. **Networking and Relationships:** Bill Gates teaches that business is fundamentally about relationships. He stresses the importance of building and maintaining a solid network and teaches practical skills for networking effectively.

9. **Customer-Centric Approach:** Gates advocates for a customer-centric business approach. He teaches that understanding customer needs and exceeding their expectations is at the heart of business growth and retention.

10. **Life-Long Learning:** Finally, Gates champions the concept of lifelong learning. He encourages continuous personal and professional development, stressing that the business landscape is ever evolving and requires continual adaptation and learning.

§

Bill Gates is celebrated as a business teacher for his unique ability to distill lessons from his vast real-world experience and innovative mindset. His teachings emphasize data-driven strategies, ethical responsibility, and a global perspective, making them relevant and actionable for entrepreneurs and executives alike. Gates highlights the importance of adaptability, leadership development, and relationship-building as key drivers of success while advocating for customer-centric approaches and lifelong learning. Together, these principles form a comprehensive blueprint for navigating the complexities of the business world.

BOB CHAPMAN

Because I am the host and the executive producer of Live with the Famous Dr AL, The Doctor of Positivity and Happiness, I have access to some of the greatest minds in the world. I heard of Bob Chapman when I read Simon Sinek's Leaders Eat Last. I immediately reached out to him.

Bob Chapman, Chairman and CEO of Barry-Wehmiller, is renowned for his entrepreneurial acumen and revolutionary approach to business leadership. Grounded in a philosophy he calls "Truly Human Leadership," Chapman's principles are a clarion call for transformation in the corporate world. In the voice of a seasoned business writer, let us delve into the ten principles at the core of Chapman's teachings, each underpinning a model that redefines success in the business realm.

1. **People are Precious Beings:** Central to Chapman's leadership philosophy is that employees are not merely resources but inherently valuable beings whose well-being is crucial. This view compels leaders to nurture, respect, and care for their employees, recognizing that each person's contribution goes beyond mere labor to the human aspect of their lives.

2. **Emphasizing Empathetic Leadership:** Chapman champions the cause of empathy in leadership, asserting that understanding

and sharing the feelings of another is a powerful catalyst for employee engagement and loyalty. Chapman's method cultivates a supportive and understanding workplace culture by encouraging leaders to adopt the perspective of their employees.

3. **Leadership as Stewardship:** Under Chapman's guidance, leadership transcends traditional boundaries of corporate governance and evolves into stewardship. This principle advocates for leaders to act as caretakers of their employees' overall well-being, fostering personal and professional growth within the organization.

4. **The Power of Listening Effective Communication:** Communication is a two-way street, with listening as important as speaking. Chapman strongly emphasizes the power of listening, urging leaders to truly hear and consider employee input as a critical element of decision-making and innovation.

5. **Visionary Thinking for a Better World:** Chapman encourages leaders to look beyond profit margins and shareholder value to how their companies can improve the world. This involves setting visionary goals that align business objectives with societal improvement, thus driving a purpose-driven approach to business operations.

6. **Building Trust Through Transparency:** Transparency is another pillar of Chapman's leadership model. He posits that openness in operations and decision-making builds employee trust, fostering a more cooperative and transparent workplace environment. Trust is seen as a value and a strategic asset.

7. **Cultivating a Culture of Celebration:** Recognition and celebration are integral to maintaining morale and motivation at work. Chapman advises that leaders should consistently acknowledge and celebrate the efforts and successes of their teams, whether through small acknowledgments or large-scale commemorations. This reinforces a positive feedback loop and encourages a culture of appreciation.

8. **Ensuring Safety and Security:** Physical, emotional, and psychological safety are paramount in Chapman's framework. He argues that ensuring a safe working environment is a fundamental responsibility of any leader, crucial not only for compliance and productivity but also for fostering an environment where employees feel genuinely cared for.

9. **Focus on Community and Family:** Chapman's principles extend to creating a sense of community and familial support within the workplace. He believes that organizations should support employees and their families, recognizing that a supportive family environment enhances employee satisfaction and performance.

10. **Commitment to Continuous Improvement:** Chapman does not view any of his principles as checkmarks on a corporate to-do list but as continuous commitments. He advocates for ongoing improvement in leadership practices, organizational culture, and personal development, emphasizing that the journey of Truly Human Leadership is never complete.

§

In synthesizing these tenets, Bob Chapman offers more than just a leadership strategy; he proposes a philosophical shift in how businesses operate, and leaders lead. His principles challenge the traditional corporate focus on the bottom line to consider the human element at every level of operation. As businesses worldwide seek to navigate a rapidly changing landscape, Chapman's Truly Human Leadership provides a beacon for creating more prosperous and compassionate enterprises. In an era searching for meaning and authenticity, Chapman's voice stands out, urging leaders to consider the legacy they leave in the lives of those they lead.

STEPHEN R. COVEY

Steven R. Covey's "The 7 Habits of Highly Effective People" is a personal and professional development landmark that remains as relevant today as when it was first published. His principles have inspired millions to reevaluate their approach to life and work. While Covey's core work centers around seven habits, exploring an expanded set of ten provides a more in-depth understanding of his philosophy.

Let's journey through these principles, reassured of their continued effectiveness in today's dynamic business environment.

1. **Be Proactive:** Covey's first principle, "Be Proactive," is foundational. It emphasizes the importance of taking responsibility for our own lives. In a business context, this entails taking initiative and thinking ahead. For instance, a proactive leader might anticipate a potential supply chain disruption and take steps to mitigate it before it occurs. They recognize that they are the architects of their fate and encourage their teams to take charge of their tasks with ownership and responsibility.

2. **Begin with the End in Mind:** This principle urges us to envision the desired outcome from the very start. For business leaders, this means setting clear, strategic goals and ensuring that every action aligns with these objectives. Whether it is a product launch or an annual business plan, beginning with the end in mind provides a roadmap and sets a clear direction for the entire team.

3. **Put First Things First:** Prioritization is crucial in business. "Put First Things First" teaches us to distinguish between what is urgent and what is essential. Influential leaders manage their time and resources by focusing on activities that align with their core goals and delegating or delaying less critical tasks.

4. **Think Win-Win:** Covey advocates for a cooperative rather than a competitive approach. In business, this means fostering an environment where all parties can succeed. The best leaders negotiate deals and create strategies that offer value to all stakeholders, believing that the success of one can propel the success of others.

5. **Seek First to Understand, Then to Be Understood:** Communication is vital in any business. This principle involves empathetic listening that leads to deeper understanding. Leaders who practice this can effectively address concerns and build a strong rapport with their team and clients, resulting in more efficient strategy execution.

6. **Synergize:** The concept of synergy implies that the whole is greater than the sum of its parts. This means fostering collaboration among diverse team members to produce superior results in a business setting. It's about leveraging individual strengths and compensating for weaknesses through teamwork.

7. **Sharpen the Saw:** Personal and professional upkeep is vital for sustained success. "Sharpen the Saw" emphasizes the importance of continuous improvement and balance. Visionary business leaders encourage their teams to pursue personal development and maintain physical, mental, and emotional health, which boosts productivity and job satisfaction.

8. **Find Your Voice:** Covey encourages finding one's unique voice as a principle by expanding on his original habits. This means discovering and leveraging your unique value proposition in the market. Leaders who find their voice are more authentic and can effectively inspire their teams.

9. **Inspire Others to Find Their Voice:** Great leaders find their own voice and inspire their teams to find theirs. This principle is about empowering others. Leaders can build a more competent and motivated workforce by encouraging team members to identify and use their unique strengths

10. **Balance Courage with Consideration:** In business negotiations and decisions, it is essential to strike a balance between courage and consideration. This principle teaches us to be assertive, confident in our convictions, and respectful and empathetic towards others. This balance can result in more productive relationships and outcomes.

§

Incorporating these ten principles, initially propagated or inspired by Covey, into daily business practice can significantly enhance personal effectiveness and organizational performance. However, it's important to note that applying these principles in a dynamic business environment can be challenging. For example, balancing courage with consideration might be difficult in high-pressure negotiations. Yet, they encourage a holistic approach, emphasizing professional success, personal fulfillment, and ethical conduct. Adopting Covey's framework can transform business strategies and the cultures within which these strategies are implemented. As we navigate the complexities of modern business environments, Covey's timeless wisdom remains a guiding light.

STEPHEN M.R. COVEY

Again, because of my role as the host and the executive director of Live with the Famous Dr. AL, I have access to some of the greatest minds. One is Steven M.R. Covey, Steven R. Covey's son. He and his father share a passion for teaching.

As one of the world's best business teachers, I'm often asked about the luminaries in the field who have not only shaped their enterprises but also transformed the way we think about leadership and management. Steven M.R. Covey is a beacon of innovative thought and ethical leadership among these influential figures. His profound insights and practical approaches to business and life resonate with anyone aspiring to make a meaningful impact. Below, I will outline why Steven M.R. Covey is highly regarded and share ten of his most pivotal teachings.

Here is why Steven M.R. Covey is a Great Business Teacher:

1. **Foundations in Trust:** Covey revolutionized business leadership with a simple yet profound principle: trust is the very basis of the modern economy and effective leadership. Trust is not merely a soft, social virtue but a measurable accelerator to organizational success. Covey's emphasis on trust transcends business theories; it's a practical strategy embedded within all his teachings.

2. **Academic Rigor and Practical Application:** With an MBA from Harvard Business School and extensive experience as a leading practitioner of corporate success strategies, Covey brings an impeccable blend of academic rigor and practical wisdom to his teachings. This combination enriches his credibility and makes his concepts universally applicable, from small teams to multinational corporations.

3. **Legacy of Leadership:** As the son of Stephen R. Covey, the legendary author of The 7 Habits of Highly Effective People, Steven M.R. Covey grew up in an environment steeped in leadership principles. He has built upon this legacy, continuing to evolve the conversation about effective management and leadership in the 21st century.

4. **Global Influence:** Covey's influence extends across the globe through his books, such as The Speed of Trust, which has been translated into multiple languages and has sold millions of copies worldwide. This highlights the universal applicability and importance of trust and integrity in all human endeavors.

5. **A Holistic Approach:** Covey teaches that business effectiveness requires a holistic approach that includes personal integrity, character, and intention. His work emphasizes that how leaders behave—and inspire behavior in others—ripples outward to affect entire organizations.

Ten Pivotal Teachings of Steven M.R. Covey

1. **Build Trust from the Inside Out:** Covey teaches that trust begins within each individual and radiates outward. Personal credibility is the foundation upon which we build all other forms of trust.

2. **The Five Waves of Trust:** According to Covey, trust operates in five waves: self, relationship, organizational, market, and societal. Understanding these waves helps leaders diagnose and improve trust at all levels.

3. **Trust is a Function of Character and Competence:** He emphasizes that trustworthiness stems from character (integrity and intent) and competence (capabilities and results). Leaders must cultivate both to be truly effective.

4. **The 13 Behaviors of High-Trust Leaders:** Covey outlines behaviors that high-trust leaders exhibit, such as talking straight, demonstrating respect, creating transparency, righting wrongs, and showing loyalty.

5. **Speed and Cost of Trust:** One of Covey's core principles is that trust increases speed and reduces costs in all interactions and transactions, making organizations more profitable and relationships more robust.

6. **Leading with Trust in Times of Change:** Covey argues that trust becomes even more critical in times of change, as it reduces resistance and increases engagement and innovation.

7. **The Economic Value of Trust:** He quantifies trust economically, showing how high-trust organizations achieve better outcomes, greater loyalty, and, ultimately, more robust financial performance.

8. **Trust and Collaboration:** Trust is essential for effective collaboration, which is increasingly important in a globalized business environment where cross-cultural teamwork is joint.

9. **Rebuilding Trust:** Covey provides a framework for recovering from trust breaches, focusing on sincerity, accountability, and taking steps to make amends.

10. **Extending Smart Trust:** He advocates for 'Smart Trust,' a balanced approach that optimizes the benefits of trust with the necessary risk management. He recognizes the importance of character and analysis in trusting others.

§

I believe embracing Steven M.R. Covey's teachings can significantly alter the course of your leadership journey. His emphasis on trust and integrity fosters a healthier organizational culture and builds a resilient, innovative, and highly collaborative business environment. As we integrate these lessons into our practices, we contribute to a legacy of sustainable and effective leadership that can carry forth into all areas of life.

JAIREK ROBBINS

I also met Jairek Robbins, head of Success magazine, because of Live with the Famous Dr. AL. Jairek Robbins, a renowned performance coach and motivational speaker, has significantly contributed to personal development and peak performance strategies. His teachings, deeply influenced by his experiences and his father, Tony Robbins, blend a practical approach with profound insights to guide individuals and businesses toward success. Here, we explore ten core principles that Robbins advocates, each a cornerstone for achieving professional excellence and fostering personal growth.

1. **Clarity of Vision:** Robbins emphasizes the importance of having a clear vision. He teaches that clarity in one's goals, desires, and purpose is pivotal for effectively directing efforts and resources. This principle is about defining success on your own terms and setting a precise path to achieve it. Knowing where you want to go isn't enough; you also need to understand why that destination matters to you.

2. **Embrace the Power of Learning:** Continual learning is at the heart of Robbins' philosophy. He believes that the pursuit of knowledge and the willingness to acquire new skills are essential for staying relevant and competitive in today's fast-paced world. Robbins encourages embracing formal education and life experiences as opportunities to grow, urging his followers to remain students of life, perpetually curious, and open to new ideas.

3. **Develop Robust Health and Energy:** Robbins teaches that personal vitality and health are foundational to achieving one's best performance. He advocates for a balanced lifestyle, including regular physical activity, a nutritional diet, and adequate rest. This principle is based on the premise that a healthy body supports a healthy mind, thus enabling individuals to operate at their peak.

4. **Effective Time Management:** According to Robbins, time management is crucial. He instructs his clients to prioritize tasks and focus on what truly moves the needle. This involves distinguishing between being 'busy' and being 'productive' and eliminating timewasters from one's daily routine. Robbins' strategies often include planning and delegation as key tools for freeing time to focus on high-impact activities. These practical strategies can empower you to take control of your time and productivity.

5. **Cultivate Emotional Intelligence:** Robbins strongly emphasizes the development of emotional intelligence. Understanding and managing one's emotions and empathizing with others are skills he identifies as critical for leadership and personal satisfaction. This principle is about navigating interpersonal relationships more effectively and making logical and emotionally sound decisions.

6. **Master the Art of Communication:** Effective communication is another pillar of Robbins' teachings. He believes clear, assertive communication can resolve conflicts, build trust, and foster strong relationships in personal as well as work environments. This includes verbal exchanges and non-verbal cues, listening skills, and the ability to tailor messages to different audiences.

7. **Financial Acumen:** Financial literacy is essential for personal and business success. Robbins teaches practical skills for managing personal finances, such as budgeting, investing, and

financial planning. He stresses the importance of understanding money dynamics to make informed decisions that secure financial well-being and support one's life goals.

8. **Resilience and Adaptability:** Robbins highlights resilience as a critical trait of successful individuals. He teaches strategies to cope with setbacks and challenges, advocating for a mindset that views failures as learning opportunities. Adaptability and resilience go hand-in-hand, preparing one to pivot when circumstances change and sustaining progress toward goals.

9. **Building and Leveraging Relationships:** According to Robbins, success is seldom a solo endeavor. Building a network of supportive, stimulating relationships is crucial. He instructs on cultivating meaningful, mutually beneficial connections and leveraging these relationships to achieve personal and professional objectives.

10. **Contribution and Impact:** Finally, Robbins believes in the value of having a positive impact. This principle revolves around contributing to something larger than oneself through philanthropy, mentorship, or leadership. It's about leaving a legacy that reflects one's values and desires to make a difference in the world.

§

Jairek Robbins' ten principles provide a road map for transient success and a fulfilling, balanced life. His holistic approach ensures that individuals are equipped with the strategies for achieving their goals, as well as the wisdom to enjoy the journey and the fruits of their labor. As we distill these lessons, we find a blueprint for professional excellence and personal happiness, a testament to Robbins' profound understanding of human potential and success.

SIMON SINEK

Simon Sinek, a visionary thinker and leadership guru, has dramatically reshaped the conversation around corporate leadership and management philosophy. His ideas, especially those articulated in his influential book Leaders Eat Last, have provided a profound blueprint for modern leadership. His philosophy, deeply rooted in the biological and anthropological imperatives that drive human behavior, suggests that the most effective leaders prioritize their teams' well-being.

Sinek's central thesis in Leaders Eat Last revolves around the concept that great leaders create environments where people feel safe, where they feel that their leaders would sacrifice their own comfort—even their own survival—for the good of those in their care. This ethos is powerfully symbolized in the military tradition that inspired the book's title: leaders eat last. Many of the world's most respected military organizations follow this tradition, which requires officers to wait until their subordinates are served before eating. This practice isn't just about food; it's a profound statement about leadership priorities, signaling the team that their needs come first.

At the heart of Sinek's philosophy is the 'Circle of Safety' idea. This concept explains that in environments where individuals feel protected and supported by their leadership, they are more likely to innovate, collaborate, and take beneficial risks. Conversely, in environments where individuals feel vulnerable or under threat, they are likely to become more conservative and self-protective, behaviors that ultimately stymie growth and innovation.

Sinek posits that the role of a leader is akin to that of a caregiver. By creating a secure atmosphere, leaders liberate their teams from internal competition that can sabotage cooperation and collective success. He frequently draws on biological mechanisms to underscore his points, explaining how hormones like endorphins, dopamine, serotonin, and oxytocin influence workplace interactions and feelings of well-being. For instance, individuals who are convinced that their leaders have their best interests at heart and feel a strong personal connection to their group release serotonin and oxytocin, which are frequently linked to feelings of trust and loyalty.

Another crucial aspect of Sinek's approach is his emphasis on the 'why' of a business—the core purpose or belief that inspires people to do their best work. This aspect is consistent with his earlier work, notably presented in his book Start With Why, where he argues that understanding and communicating the 'why' is crucial for any organization's long-term success. By connecting employees' everyday tasks to a greater purpose, leaders can foster a more engaged and motivated workforce.

Sinek's philosophy fundamentally challenges the conventional wisdom of cutthroat corporate practices, where financial gain justifies nearly any means. He argues that such short-term thinking jeopardizes the long-term health of an organization. Sustainable success, he suggests, comes from cultivating trust and cooperation among workers. The proof, he notes, is evident in companies that have embraced these principles, which often outperform their peers significantly in the long term.

Sinek's insights are particularly relevant in the context of modern challenges such as digital transformation and global competition. In these arenas, companies face not only the traditional pressures of the market, but also new stresses related to technological disruption and rapid change. Sinek suggests that in such times, the principles of trust and safety are more vital than ever. Companies that can maintain a stable, supportive core in the face of external pressures are better positioned to adapt and thrive.

Moreover, Sinek is a staunch advocate for ethical leadership. He contends that the practice of leaders eating last is more than just securing loyalty or improving morale; it is also a moral imperative. According to Sinek, the true test of leadership is not just whether it leads to success but whether it contributes to the welfare of all stakeholders—from employees and customers to the broader community and the environment.

§

In summary, Simon Sinek's business philosophy offers a powerful and humane approach to leadership, which is desperately needed in today's often impersonal and cutthroat business environments. His advocacy for a leadership style that emphasizes safety, trust, and the importance of a clear and compelling 'why' presents a clear and persuasive blueprint for building organizations that are not only successful but also sustainable and nurturing for the people within them. By urging leaders to eat last, Sinek isn't just recommending a practice but a paradigm shift in how we think about and enact leadership in the 21st century.

MOHAMMED BIN RASHID

Mohammed bin Rashid Al Maktoum, the Vice President and Prime Minister of the United Arab Emirates and the ruler of Dubai, is a visionary leader whose principles and insights into governance, business, and leadership have transformed Dubai while also providing valuable lessons for global leadership.

His strategic vision is encapsulated in numerous speeches and writings, notably in his book "My Vision: Challenges in the Race for Excellence." The principles he teaches can be categorized into several core areas: visionary leadership, innovation and development, embracing change, and humanitarianism.

1. **Visionary Leadership**

    One of the most striking aspects of Mohammed bin Rashid Al Maktoum's approach is his emphasis on visionary leadership. He believes a leader's primary role is to forge the future rather than just administer over the present. He famously said, "The word 'impossible' is not in leaders' dictionaries. No matter how big the challenges, strong faith, determination, and resolve will overcome them." This saying reflects his philosophy that leaders must be creators of circumstance, not creatures of it.

    His leadership style underscores the importance of setting high goals. He contends that setting mediocre goals is a common trap: "Most people aim at nothing in life and hit it with remarkable accuracy." His own leadership journey exemplifies this principle, having transformed Dubai from a modest port city into a global metropolis known for its skyscrapers, business-friendly environment, and technological innovations.

2. Innovation and Development

Mohammed bin Rashid Al Maktoum is synonymous with the word 'innovation'. He sees innovation as a fundamental principle that applies to all aspects of governance and business, not just technology. "Innovation is not an option but a necessity. It is not a culture but a business practice," he asserts. For him, innovation is the tool through which modern challenges are faced and turned into opportunities.

This principle is evident in initiatives like Dubai Smart City, where the integration of technology into urban management creates efficiencies and improves the quality of life for residents and visitors. His approach to innovation is systemic, advocating for policies that support sustainable development and attract world-class talent.

3. Embracing Change

A key lesson from Mohammed bin Rashid Al Maktoum's leadership is his approach to change. He once stated, "Change or you will be changed: as we see from companies that were once untouchable but disappeared with the advent of technology." His tenure as ruler of Dubai and Prime Minister of the UAE has been marked by significant structural changes in economic policies, leading to a diversification away from oil dependency.

His proactive stance on change is about anticipation and preparation. This principle is not just about adapting to change but about leading it, ensuring that Dubai and the UAE are always ahead of the curve in terms of economic trends and shifts.

4. Humanitarianism

Despite his focus on business and development, Mohammed bin Rashid Al Maktoum consistently emphasizes the importance of humanitarianism. He believes that a nation's prosperity is hollow without its people's well-being. This is reflected in his statement, *"A great leader creates more great leaders and does not reduce the institution to a single person."* He views true success as a shared endeavor—an achievement that uplifts the community as a whole.

Philanthropy is an integral part of his leadership philosophy, demonstrated through initiatives like the Mohammed bin Rashid Al Maktoum Global Initiatives, which aims to combat poverty and disease, spread knowledge, empower communities, and foster innovation across the Arab world.

§

The leadership principles taught by Mohammed bin Rashid Al Maktoum apply far beyond Dubai's borders or the corridors of governmental power. They are vital for anyone who aspires to lead in the modern world, characterized by rapid changes and unprecedented challenges. His belief in the power of vision, the necessity of innovation, the imperative of embracing change, and the importance of humanitarian values form the cornerstone of his enduring legacy. As he succinctly puts it, "The race for excellence has no finish line." These principles define his leadership and encourage a continuous pursuit of excellence that can inspire all leaders and aspiring leaders worldwide.

MARK VICTOR HANSEN

Through my show, I met Mark Victor Hansen and his wife Crystal, who've appeared with me often. Mark is best known as the co-creator of the Chicken Soup for the Soul series, and is a prolific motivational speaker and author whose teachings have inspired millions.

In distilling his philosophy, we discover a wealth of practical advice that applies not only to personal development but also to thriving in the business world. His lessons blend motivational rhetoric, practical strategies, and anecdotal evidence, all aimed at empowering individuals to achieve their full potential. They include:

1. **Embrace an Entrepreneurial Spirit**

   At the heart of Hansen's teachings is the entrepreneurial spirit—encouraging individuals to see opportunities where others see obstacles. He believes that entrepreneurship is more than simply starting a business; it is also about thinking creatively and taking the initiative in any context. Hansen often emphasizes the importance of self-belief and vision in the entrepreneurial journey, suggesting that these elements are crucial for overcoming the fear of failure that usually impedes progress.

2. **The Power of Goal Setting**

   Hansen champions the power of goal setting as a tool to achieve business success. He advises that goals should be **SMART**:

Specific, Measurable, Achievable, Relevant, and Time-bound. By setting clear goals, individuals and organizations can create a roadmap to success, making tracking progress and maintaining motivation easier. Hansen often discusses how goals act as a catalyst for personal and professional growth, pushing individuals to go beyond their comfort zones.

3. **Cultivating Relationships**

   Networking and relationship-building are central themes in Hansen's advice. He argues that success in business often hinges on one's ability to cultivate and maintain strong relationships. Hansen teaches that genuine interest in others, coupled with a willingness to help without expecting anything in return, lays the foundation for robust networks that can open doors to opportunities that would otherwise remain closed.

4. **The Importance of Resilience**

   Resilience is another cornerstone of Hansen's philosophy. In his view, setbacks are not failures but steppingstones to success. He underscores the importance of persistence and adaptability, encouraging entrepreneurs to view every challenge as an opportunity to learn and grow. Hansen's own career—particularly his experiences of rejection before the phenomenal success of Chicken Soup for the Soul—is a testament to the power of resilience.

5. **Continuous Learning and Innovation**

   Hansen is a staunch advocate for lifelong learning and continuous innovation. He believes that the business landscape is constantly evolving and that staying informed and adaptable is key to maintaining a competitive advantage. This involves keeping abreast of industry trends and continuously seeking personal and professional development opportunities. According to Hansen, innovation is not about reinventing the wheel but rather about making incremental improvements that collectively make a significant impact.

6. Leveraging the Power of Visualization

Visualization is a technique Hansen often discusses. He encourages individuals to visualize their success vividly, arguing that doing so helps to align subconscious and conscious minds towards achieving set goals. Hansen believes that visualization not only motivates but also activates creative thinking and problem-solving abilities, which are crucial in navigating the complexities of business.

7. Giving Back

Philanthropy is integral to Hansen's vision of business success. He posits that the most successful individuals are those who give back to their communities and make a positive impact on the world. This principle is reflected in his life through his extensive charitable work. For Hansen, giving back is not only a moral obligation but also a vital component of personal fulfillment and success.

Hansen was the celebrated co-author with Jack Canfield of the transformative 'Chicken Soup for the Soul' series. His insights are not mere guidelines but transformative tools for personal growth and success.

I'll explore ten of Hansen's most impactful principles, a journey of profound transformation, engaging readers in powerful and inspiring personal and professional growth.

1. The Art of Asking

Hansen champions the power of inquiry with his principle that "the answer is always no if you don't ask." He encourages individuals to step beyond their comfort zones and ask for what they need, whether it's resources, information, or connections. This principle highlights that opportunities are seized through active asking rather than passive waiting.

2. **Envision Your Future**

   Visualization is a key principle for Hansen. He advocates vividly imagining your desired future—seeing, feeling, and experiencing it before it happens. This practice creates a mental and emotional alignment that propels you toward your goals. This is more than daydreaming; it's a strategic practice for setting the stage for real-world achievements.

3. **Embrace a Positive Vision**

   Building on the power of visualization, Hansen stresses the importance of maintaining a positive outlook. He posits that a positive vision acts as a beacon, guiding through adversity and illuminating possibilities in times of challenge. This mindset encourages resilience and an openness to see potential growth in every situation.

4. **Set Specific Goals**

   Hansen underscores the importance of setting specific, clear goals. However, he strongly emphasizes the specificity and clarity of these goals. For Hansen, well-defined goals are not just aspirations but actionable and measurable steps to achieve tangible results. This practical approach empowers individuals, making success feel within reach.

5. **Cultivate Unwavering Belief**

   Hansen underscores the necessity of unwavering belief in one's capabilities and the feasibility of one's goals. This principle involves cultivating a deep-seated belief that what you are working towards is possible and inevitable. Such belief is not only motivating but also attracts support from others.

6. **Foster Relationships**

   Hansen advocates strongly for the development of social capital. Success is rarely a solo endeavor; instead, it's supported by a network of relationships. Building trust and collaboration across personal and professional networks can provide a critical support system and open doors that might otherwise remain close.

7. **Continuous Learning**

   A hallmark of Hansen's philosophy is the commitment to lifelong learning. He suggests constant intellectual and experiential growth is essential to staying relevant and practical. By remaining students of life, we ensure that our skills and knowledge continue to evolve as our environments change.

8. **Leverage the Power of Generosity**

   Generosity, according to Hansen, is a powerful tool for success. By giving generously—whether time, resources, or knowledge—you build a foundation of reciprocity and goodwill. Generosity enhances one's reputation and builds an enduring legacy.

9. **Perseverance Through Challenges**

   Perseverance is crucial in the face of adversity. Hansen's teachings focus on resilience, viewing challenges as stepping stones rather than obstacles. Each challenge offers lessons and opportunities for growth.

10. **Celebrate Your Successes and Learn from Failures**

    Hansen underlines the significance of acknowledging and celebrating one's achievements, no matter how small. This principle is complemented by a resilient approach to failures, viewing them as invaluable learning opportunities, fostering a mindset that values progress, continuous improvement, and a source of encouragement and resilience in the face of challenges.

§

Mark Victor Hansen's principles are not just guidelines but a transformative roadmap for those seeking to elevate their lives and careers. His teachings focus not solely on achieving success but on creating a life of meaning and impact. The most adept business writers would describe Hansen's message not as a guide for personal achievement but as a strategic approach to cultivating a fulfilling and rewarding professional journey. When embraced wholeheartedly, these principles become potent catalysts for surpassing personal and professional goals, propelling individuals toward a life of significance and success. These teachings provide a comprehensive guide to personal and business success. His approach combines motivational advice with practical strategies, underpinned by a profound understanding of human psychology and market dynamics. For anyone looking to thrive in the modern business environment, Hansen's lessons offer a blueprint for developing the resilience, creativity, and strategic thinking necessary to excel. Through his words, we learn that success is more than just achieving personal or financial goals; it is also about making a positive difference in the world.

JACK CANFIELD

Jack Canfield, celebrated for his transformative insights into personal development and peak performance, epitomizes the ethos of American success in the self-help and business realms. I met Jack because of Steve Harrison. I went to his house to be mentored in writing my intended best-selling book, The Secrets to Living a Fantastic Life. Jack was so impressed that he wrote the foreword for the book.

Jack's teachings, which span decades, offer a blueprint for personal achievement and a guiding compass for countless entrepreneurs and business professionals seeking fulfillment and success in their endeavors.

A cornerstone of Canfield's philosophy is the emphasis on goal setting and vision. His belief in the power of setting clear, actionable objectives is encapsulated in the principle that "whatever you can conceive and believe, you can achieve." This mantra, which echoes through his works, particularly in "The Success Principles," offers a structured approach to turning abstract dreams into tangible realities. Canfield stresses the importance of vividly visualizing one's goals, suggesting that this mental imagery acts as a catalyst for action, propelling the individual towards achievement through a combination of desire, belief, and persistence.

Canfield's teachings also heavily advocate for responsibility. He argues that taking 100% responsibility for one's life is the first step toward creating the life one desires. This principle challenges individuals to shift their perspective from blame to ownership of outcomes, including failures and successes. Canfield's directive encourages a proactive stance on life, urging individuals to seize control over their circumstances by reacting constructively to adversities and setbacks. This attitude reshapes how one perceives and interacts with the world, fostering resilience and a proactive mindset crucial for business success.

Another significant aspect of Canfield's methodology is the power of positive thinking and affirmations. He posits that one's thoughts dictate the trajectory of one's life, where positive thoughts lead to positive outcomes. By regularly affirming one's aspirations and maintaining a positive mindset, Canfield believes individuals can influence their environment and attract success. This belief aligns with the principles of the Law of Attraction, a concept he popularized with his co-authoring of "Chicken Soup for the Soul," which illustrates how a positive outlook can transform personal and professional lives through myriad stories.

Networking and building relationships are also pivotal in Canfield's framework. He underscores the necessity of surrounding oneself with a network of supportive, ambitious individuals who can offer guidance, support, and insight. This network is not only a source of motivation but also a critical resource pool that can propel an individual towards their goals. Canfield's emphasis on mentorship and continuous learning within these networks fosters an environment where ongoing personal and professional development is highly encouraged.

Furthermore, Canfield's approach to challenges and failure is particularly instructive for business professionals. He teaches that obstacles should not be viewed as insurmountable barriers but as opportunities to learn and grow. This reframing is vital in a business context where setbacks are inevitable and often serve as steppingstones to greater success. Canfield's perspective helps individuals cultivate resilience, a quality that is critical to maintaining momentum in the volatile business world.

In addition to these principles, Canfield's dedication to continuous improvement, or what the Japanese call "Kaizen," is a testament to his commitment to lifelong learning and excellence. He advocates for regular self-assessment and feedback gathering as tools to continually refine one's approach and strategies. In a business landscape that is constantly evolving, this commitment to iteration and refinement is crucial, as it necessitates adaptability and a willingness to embrace change.

Canfield's teachings extend beyond individual success by encouraging a holistic view of achievement that includes giving back to the community and fostering an environment where others can also succeed. This broader perspective on success aligns closely with contemporary views on corporate social responsibility and ethical leadership in the business world.

In synthesizing these principles, Jack Canfield offers not just a set of tools for personal and professional development but a philosophy that can be woven into the fabric of one's life and work. His teachings encourage a balanced approach to success, emphasizing ethical conduct, personal responsibility, and the importance of social networks, all underpinned by a positive mindset and a clear vision. For business professionals and entrepreneurs, Canfield's insights are inspirational and instrumental in crafting a path to sustainable success and fulfillment in their careers and beyond.

In the ever-evolving business landscape, a transformative approach reshapes the foundation of entrepreneurial success and corporate leadership. Dubbed "The New Paradigm: To Get - Give First," this philosophy champions the ethos of generosity and reciprocity as the cornerstone of business strategy. By prioritizing giving over receiving, companies are discovering that they can enhance their prosperity and foster a more collaborative and sustainable business environment.

At the heart of this paradigm is a simple yet profound inversion of traditional business logic: instead of focusing solely on what can be gained, the emphasis shifts towards what can be given first. This approach is not entirely altruistic; rather, it is a strategic maneuver designed to build trust, strengthen relationships, and, ultimately, enhance the giver's long-term success. Beyond that, it offers a path to personal growth and fulfillment by aligning with the innate human desire to contribute and make a positive impact. The principle is based on the understanding that in today's interconnected world, the success of one entity is often intrinsically linked to the well-being of its community and stakeholders.

1. **Building Trust and Credibility**

   In an era where consumers are increasingly skeptical of corporate motives, trust has emerged as the new economy's currency. By giving first—through valuable content, superior service, or support for community initiatives—companies can establish a reputation of generosity and reliability. This attracts customers and engenders loyalty, turning customers into advocates and collaborators. For instance, companies like [Company A] and [Company B] that offer free valuable resources or services without immediate expectation of return often see a higher return on investment through increased customer loyalty and brand strength.

2. **Networking and Relationship Building**

   "Give to get" becomes particularly poignant in the context of networking. The adage "It's not what you know, but who you know" still holds, but with a twist: it's also about who trusts you. Individuals and companies can build more robust and supportive networks by approaching professional relationships with the mindset of contributing rather than extracting. This network, in turn, becomes a valuable asset, facilitating opportunities for collaboration and mutual growth that would not have arisen otherwise.

3. **Encouraging Innovation and Collaboration:**

   The New Paradigm - Give To Get

   A culture of giving encourages a more open exchange of ideas and resources, which can lead to increased innovation and efficiency. Employees, partners, and competitors are more likely to reciprocate when a company shows willingness to share knowledge, skills, and opportunities. This environment fosters a collaborative ecosystem where collective problem-solving becomes the norm, accelerating innovation and expanding the potential for new ideas and solutions.

4. **Sustainable Business Practice**

   The giving-first approach aligns closely with the principles of corporate social responsibility and sustainable business practices. Focusing on what a company can give back to the environment and society addresses the growing consumer demand for ethical business practices while also investing in its markets' long-term viability. For example, companies that prioritize eco-friendly practices or contribute to social causes are perceived favorably by environmentally and socially conscious consumers and benefit the planet and its inhabitants.

5. **Challenges and Considerations**

   However, the implementation of this paradigm is not without its challenges. It requires a shift in mindset from short-term gains to long-term goals and reevaluating success metrics. Businesses must balance their generosity with wise strategic planning to ensure their giving translates into sustainable growth. Furthermore, the risk of exploitation—wherein the initial generosity is not reciprocated—can deter firms from adopting this approach. To mitigate these concerns, companies can [specific strategy or action] to ensure a balanced and strategic approach to giving.

"The New Paradigm: To Get - Give First" represents a shift towards a more collaborative, trustworthy, and sustainable approach to business. It encourages companies to reconsider traditional competitive tactics and embrace a strategy that benefits all stakeholders. By doing so, businesses not only enhance their prospects but also contribute to a healthier economy and society, paving the way for a more prosperous and sustainable future. The paradigm, while challenging, offers a compelling blueprint for future business leaders and entrepreneurs who wish to thrive in a complex, interconnected world filled with opportunities for collective success and societal impact.

In business, where pragmatism often reigns, the power of aligning with a more significant cause is sometimes overlooked. However, modern enterprises increasingly recognize that associating with a more important reason is a moral choice and a strategic imperative. This association, often manifested through corporate social responsibility (CSR) initiatives, sustainability efforts, or philanthropic endeavors, does more than paint a company in a good light; it propels the business forward, fosters innovation, and builds a more profound connection with consumers.

6. Strategic Advantage through Differentiation

In today's highly competitive market, differentiation is crucial to survival and growth. Companies can distinguish themselves from their competitors by associating with a more significant cause. This differentiation is more than having superior products or services; it is also about embodying values that resonate deeply with consumers. According to various studies, more than half of consumers are willing to pay more for products from brands committed to positive social and environmental impact. By aligning with meaningful causes, businesses can tap into this growing consumer base that prioritizes ethical considerations in purchasing decisions.

7. **Enhanced Brand Loyalty and Reputation**

   When a company commits to a more significant cause, it often sees a direct impact on its brand loyalty. Customers tend to return to brands that meet their needs and reflect their values. The consumers' loyalty is strengthened when they see consistent and genuine commitment rather than one-off charity drives or superficial campaigns. Moreover, in the age of social media, where every action a company takes can be instantly scrutinized, a sustained commitment to a cause can protect and enhance a company's reputation, turning potential crises into opportunities to demonstrate corporate values in action.

8. **Attracting and Retaining Talent**

   Today's workforce, particularly among millennials and Gen Z, seeks more than just employment; they are increasingly driven by purpose and seek out workplaces that reflect their values. By associating with a more significant cause, companies can attract top talent who are skilled and passionately committed to their roles, knowing their work contributes to the greater good. Employees who feel more connected and engaged with their employer's mission may have lower turnover rates, increased satisfaction, and higher productivity.

9. **Innovation and Longevity**

   Associating with a more prominent cause pushes companies to innovate by forcing them to solve complex problems that matter. This might entail developing new, more sustainable production methods, adopting greener technologies, or finding efficient ways to give back to the community. Such innovations can lead to discoveries that refine a company's offerings and create new markets or product lines. Furthermore, companies are more likely to think long-term in their strategic planning by focusing on long-term challenges, paving the way for sustainability and longevity in an ever-evolving market landscape.

10. Building Community and Stakeholder Trust

Businesses do not operate in vacuums; they are integral to their communities. By associating with a more significant cause, a company demonstrates its commitment to the well-being of its community, which can generate immense goodwill and trust among stakeholders. This trust is especially crucial during times of crisis when the community's support can significantly affect how a company weathers adversity.

11. Regulatory and Government Favor

Governments and regulatory bodies worldwide increasingly impose regulations favoring socially and environmentally responsible companies. By taking the lead in these areas, businesses can ensure compliance and benefit from government incentives like tax breaks, grants, and other supports. Moreover, companies regarded as CSR leaders often influence industry standards and regulations, positioning themselves as pioneers in new, regulated markets.

§

As Canfield teaches us, the importance of associating with a more significant cause transcends the feel-good factor or marketing benefit; it is a multifaceted strategic asset that can drive a business to new heights of success and relevance. It aligns with the shifting global expectations of corporate conduct and responds to the growing consumer demand for brands with a conscience. In this new business era, the most successful companies will act as forces for good, integrating their profit motives with the broader social and environmental contexts in which they operate. This is not only good ethics but also a sound business strategy.

PERRY MARSHALL

My friend Perry Marshall has taught me a lot about business since we met at a Dan Kennedy mastermind decades ago. Here are some things you need to know about Perry and his teaching

Perry Marshall is a renowned business consultant, author, and speaker who teaches entrepreneurs and business owners how to achieve significant growth and profitability through advanced marketing strategies. His teachings revolve around several key principles and methodologies that have proven effective across various industries. Here is an overview of what Perry Marshall teaches:

1. **80/20 Principle (Pareto Principle):** One of Perry Marshall's core teachings is the 80/20 Principle, also known as the Pareto Principle. This principle states that 80% of the results come from 20% of the efforts. Marshall emphasizes the importance of identifying and focusing on the most productive activities, customers, and products. By doing so, businesses can maximize their efficiency and profitability. He encourages entrepreneurs to continually analyze their operations to find the top 20% that generates the most significant impact and to eliminate or minimize the bottom 80% that contributes less.

2. **Direct Response Marketing:** Marshall strongly advocates direct response marketing, a strategy designed to elicit an immediate response from the target audience. Unlike traditional branding-focused marketing, direct response marketing aims to drive specific actions, such as making a purchase, signing up for a newsletter, or requesting more information. Marshall teaches how to craft compelling offers, write persuasive copy, and use powerful calls-to-action to engage prospects and convert them into customers. He believes in measuring and testing marketing campaigns to optimize performance and achieve the highest return on investment.

3. **Google AdWords and Online Advertising:** Perry Marshall is often referred to as a pioneer in the field of online advertising, particularly with Google AdWords (now Google Ads). His book, "Ultimate Guide to Google AdWords," is considered a seminal work in the industry. Marshall teaches businesses how to create effective pay-per-click (PPC) campaigns, conduct keyword research, and optimize ad performance. He emphasizes the importance of understanding the customer's intent and crafting ads that specifically address their needs and desires. By leveraging the power of Google Ads, businesses can drive targeted traffic to their websites and achieve higher conversion rates.

4. **Sales Funnels and Conversion Optimization:** Marshall stresses the importance of building effective sales funnels that guide prospects through the buying journey, starting from awareness, progressing to consideration, and finally making a decision. He teaches how to design and optimize each stage of the funnel to maximize conversions. This process includes creating lead magnets to capture email addresses, nurturing leads through email marketing, and using upsells and cross-sells to increase the average order value. By understanding the customer's journey and addressing their needs at each stage, businesses can significantly boost their sales and revenue.

5. **Guerrilla Marketing Tactics:** Perry Marshall also explores guerrilla marketing tactics, which are unconventional and low-cost marketing strategies specifically designed to achieve maximum impact. He encourages businesses to think creatively and leverage unique approaches to stand out in a crowded marketplace. These tactics often involve using social media, viral marketing, and grassroots campaigns to create buzz and attract attention. Marshall teaches how to implement these strategies effectively without breaking the bank, making them accessible to businesses of all sizes.

6. **Customer Value Optimization:** Understanding and maximizing customer value is another critical aspect of Perry Marshall's teachings. He underscores the significance of not only acquiring new customers but also nurturing and retaining existing ones. Marshall teaches how to calculate the lifetime value of a customer and use this information to make informed marketing and business decisions. By focusing on customer satisfaction, loyalty, and repeat business, companies can achieve sustainable growth and profitability.

7. **The Definitive Selling Proposition:** Marshall introduces the concept of the Definitive Selling Proposition (DSP), a unique value proposition that sets a business apart from its competitors. He teaches how to identify and articulate what makes a product or service unique and why customers should choose it over others. This process involves understanding the market, analyzing competitors, and identifying the key benefits that resonate with the target audience. A strong DSP helps businesses differentiate themselves and create a compelling reason for customers to buy.

8. **Automation and Systems:** Efficiency and scalability are crucial for business success, and Perry Marshall advocates for the use of automation and systems to achieve these goals. He teaches how to automate repetitive tasks, streamline operations, and implement systems that allow businesses to scale without compromising quality or customer service. By leveraging technology and creating efficient processes, companies can free up time and resources to focus on strategic growth initiatives.

9. **Continuous Learning and Improvement:** Finally, Perry Marshall highlights the significance of continuous learning and improvement. He advocates for entrepreneurs to remain up to date with the latest trends, technologies, and best practices in business and marketing. This operation involves investing in education, attending workshops and conferences, and constantly experimenting and testing new ideas. Marshall believes that a commitment to lifelong learning is essential for staying competitive and achieving long-term success.

§

In summary, Perry Marshall's teachings provide a comprehensive framework for businesses to achieve significant growth and profitability. By applying the 80/20 Principle, mastering direct response marketing, leveraging online advertising, optimizing sales funnels, employing guerrilla marketing tactics, maximizing customer value, creating a strong DSP, automating processes, and committing to continuous learning, entrepreneurs can transform their businesses and achieve remarkable results.

LYCKA PRINCIPLES

There are several myths about what it takes to succeed. In medical school, for example, I was taught that you must be affable, available, and able. Afterwards, I was told I had to attend the most famous achools. And buy only the most prestigious equipment. Let me dispense with those myths.

Affability

Some of the best doctors and business people I know are not that affable. They're not S.O.B.s. They're just not overly friendly.

Availability

If you are available 24/7, you never get things done. I'm available 24/7 for my wife, children and select friends. But I otherwise carefully guard my privacy.

Ability

As a doctor, you must have some ability. Same goes for businesspeople. But smart people know their weaknesses and delegate. They surround themselves with people more capable than themselves.

The best school or training program

They say you must graduate from Yale, Harvard, or Stanford. While these schools can give you a leg up, Bill Gates and Steve Jobs were university dropouts.

The most expensive equipment/premises

Not necessarily. Be selective.

And after you make it to the top, everybody will say you must have been lucky. Meanwhile, what are the keys to business success?

AUTHORITY

Authority is a critical aspect of leadership and management, playing a vital role in the success of organizations. Understanding its importance and how to achieve it is essential for anyone aspiring to lead effectively. If there is one thing, you need to be acknowledged as the "leader in your field." It's authority

The Importance of Authority

Authority, fundamentally, is the rightful power to lead, decide, and enforce obedience. It distinguishes someone who is part of a process from someone who controls it. Authority allows leaders to set goals, gather the necessary resources, and drive the organization toward success.

Authority establishes leadership: Authority is fundamental to establishing leadership within any hierarchy. It enables leaders to guide their teams and make decisions aligned with the organization's goals. Without authority, a leader's ability to enforce rules and make decisions may be compromised, potentially leading to confusion, inefficiency, and a lack of direction within the team.

Authority promotes efficiency: When leaders exercise authority effectively, they set clear expectations and delegate responsibilities, which enhances operational efficiency. Authority ensures that roles and responsibilities are well-defined, reducing overlaps and ensuring that the workforce is well-organized.

Authority ensures accountability: Authority ensures accountability by making leaders responsible for both their decisions and their outcomes. This accountability is essential for evaluating performance and implementing necessary changes.

Authority facilitates change: Adapting and changing are vital in a dynamic business environment. Leaders with authority can champion and implement change more effectively. They have the power to overcome resistance and ensure that the organization swiftly adapts to new challenges and opportunities.

How to Achieve Authority

Achieving authority is not merely about holding a position of power. It involves cultivating respect, trust, and credibility. Here are some key strategies to achieve and maintain authority, such as developing expertise in your field, building strong relationships with your team, communicating effectively, demonstrating integrity, empowering others, and being decisive in your actions. Let's delve deeper into each of these strategies.

Develop Expertise: Authority often begins with expertise. Leaders who are knowledgeable and skilled earn respect and credibility. Continuous learning and staying updated with industry trends are crucial. This expertise empowers leaders to make informed decisions and enhances their credibility.

Build Relationships: Authority is reinforced by positive relationships. Leaders who take the time to build and maintain positive relationships with their team members are more likely to be respected and followed. This involves listening, showing empathy, and being responsive to others' needs and concerns, regardless of their position or background.

Communicate Effectively: Clear and consistent communication is a cornerstone of effective leadership. Leaders must articulate their vision, the reasons behind their decisions, and the expected outcomes while being open to feedback. This helps make better decisions and strengthens team members' commitment to the leader's vision. This emphasis on communication should make you feel understood and valued, knowing that your voice and feedback are important in decision-making.

Demonstrate Integrity: A leader's actions must mirror their words. Integrity is the foundation of trust, and trust enhances authority. Leaders who consistently act ethically and transparently are more likely to be considered legitimate authorities. They set a moral compass for the organization, guiding it through prosperous and challenging times. This emphasis on integrity should reassure you of the importance of ethical leadership in building confidence within your team.

Empower Others: Authority involves empowering others by delegating responsibilities and encouraging initiative. This lightens the leader's load and helps team members grow and develop, fostering a strong sense of loyalty and commitment. This aspect of authority should inspire you to lead in a way that uplifts and motivates your team.

Be Decisive: Effective leaders make confident decisions and take responsibility for the outcomes. Indecisiveness can undermine a leader's authority and lead to uncertainty within the team. Leaders reinforce their role by being decisive and encouraging others to follow their lead.

In conclusion, authority is a pivotal element of successful leadership. It is not merely about the power to command or enforce rules but about earning respect, fostering efficiency, and driving change. Achieving authority requires expertise, relationship-building, effective communication, integrity, empowerment, and decisiveness. By cultivating these qualities, leaders can establish a solid, authoritative presence that propels the organization toward its goals. Now, it's your turn to apply these strategies in your leadership journey.

Authority and the IOFP Award

The creation of the IOFP award is a recognition of the supreme importance of authority in the business world. Bestowed on members by the IOFP, the award recognizes them as the authorities in their area of expertise. With it comes a unique Academy Award-like statue, a plaque, and one of the several crests bestowed for specific levels of inductees. Award winners are announced by a press release that features them on CNN, ABC, NBC, Telemundo, CW, and other 200 outlets.

A gala celebrates award winners accomplishments. That night they're on the red carpet, sharing the victory with friends, co-workers, employees, and family. They book early as tickets go quickly.

For full impact, awards are shared on social media. Members share the IOFP thread on their favorite social media platform. NYT bulletin boards, podcasts/syndicated radio shows, books, videos, documentaries, networking events, and all the rest of the IOFP network keep members in the spotlight as the authority in their area.

DRIVE: THE UNSEEN ENGINE OF SUCCESS

Many factors contribute to business success, from strategic planning to technological innovation. However, one of the most critical yet often overlooked elements is 'drive.' Drive is the insatiable hunger that fuels initiative. It's the "burning fire" that makes everything happen.

The Quintessence of Drive

Drive is the relentless push to achieve one's goals and the unyielding pursuit of success despite challenges and setbacks. It encompasses ambition, determination, and resilience, fueling entrepreneurs and business leaders to move forward when others might give up. While drive is intrinsic and cannot be bought or taught, it can be cultivated and harnessed to propel business ventures.

Drive: Pivotal to Business Success

1. Overcoming Adversity

   Setbacks and failures are inevitable in the tumultuous journey of business. Drive empowers individuals to rise after each fall and continue striving toward their objectives. Most successful business figures often have a history of overcoming significant adversities, with their drive transforming potential failures into steppingstones to success.

2. Sustaining Momentum

   Drive ensures that the initial enthusiasm that accompanies the launch of a business venture stays strong as challenges mount. It sustains momentum, even when the novelty wears off and the complex realities of business operations set in.

3. Fueling Innovation

   Drive is a critical ingredient for innovation. Driven individuals are not content with the status quo; they are perpetually dissatisfied and continually seek better, more efficient solutions. This restless energy fuels continuous Innovation, which is vital in a business environment where technological advancements rapidly render yesterday's innovations obsolete.

4. **Achieving High Performance**

   Drive compels individuals to perform at their highest level. It fosters a high-performance organizational culture where excellence is the norm. According to Driven, leaders inspire their teams by setting high expectations and leading by example.

5. **Attracting Opportunities**

   Drive is magnetic—it attracts opportunities. Driven individuals are proactive in seeking new opportunities and are more likely to be noticed by others who can offer opportunities such as partnerships, investments, and new ventures.

6. **Ensuring Persistence**

   Drive is synonymous with Persistence. Persistence is perhaps the most common attribute among extraordinarily successful individuals. It compels one to keep going when others have concluded that an endeavor is hopeless.

7. **Facilitating Rapid Growth**

   Drive pushes businesses to expand aggressively. Driven entrepreneurs pursue expansion, explore new markets, and capitalize on opportunities quickly and effectively.

8. **Building Resilience**

   Drive builds Resilience, enabling individuals and businesses to withstand market volatility and economic downturns. This resilience, driven by an indomitable will, is crucial for long-term business success.

9. **Enhancing Decision-Making**

   Driven individuals make decisions quickly and decisively. Their drive helps business leaders make tough decisions that others might hesitate over, which can be a critical advantage in fast-paced markets.

10. Inspiring Loyalty

Drive inspires loyalty from both customers and employees. People gravitate towards businesses driven by passion and purpose, which fosters loyalty and enhances customer retention and employee engagement.

§

Drive is the invisible force behind every successful business endeavor. It's more than a strong work ethic or passion; it's a relentless, almost stubborn resolve to achieve success despite obstacles.

Drive must be channeled effectively to foster personal success and cultivate a thriving, resilient business. Cultivate your drive, harness it, and let it propel you to heights you might never have reached otherwise. In business, as in life, drive is the difference between the ordinary and the extraordinary.

Nothing is more dangerous than a driven person without an ethical compass to steer their ship. The IOFP will help you harness your drive by surrounding you with visionary people to help you along the way.

CLARITY IN COMMUNICATION

In life and business, communicating is not just a skill; it's an imperative. Clarity fosters efficient operations, builds stakeholder trust, and sharpens the company's competitive edge.

Below, I'll explore the various reasons why clarity is crucial in business communication from the perspective of a seasoned business writer.

1. **Efficiency and Effectiveness**

   Clarity directly impacts the efficiency of business operations. Clear communication minimizes the time and resources spent on misunderstandings and corrections. When instructions, goals, or feedback are conveyed ambiguously, it often leads to costly errors and delays.

   For example, if a project manager does not outline the scope or deadlines of a project clearly, the team might miss critical objectives or waste effort on non-essential tasks. On the other hand, clear communication ensures that everyone understands their roles and responsibilities from the outset, streamlining processes and enhancing productivity.

   If you don't communicate properly, it leads to friction, arguments, and fights—often, marriages break down because of bad communication.

2. **Decision-Making**

   Clear communication is also essential in decision-making. In the fast-paced business environment, decisions must be made quickly and under pressure. Clear and concise information reduces the risk of misinterpretation and enables informed, confident decision-making. Whether it's data-driven insights or strategic directives, clarity ensures that the core message is not lost in translation, thus empowering leaders to make decisions that are in the organization's best interest.

3. **Building Trust**

   Clear communication is crucial for building and maintaining trust. Transparency and straightforwardness in business dealings, whether with employees, customers, or partners, are foundational to establishing trust. When a company communicates clearly about its policies, changes, or expectations, it leaves little room for doubt or suspicion, fostering a positive and trusting relationship. Conversely, ambiguous or deceptive communication can damage a company's reputation and lead to a loss of stakeholder trust. In a marriage, good communication facilitates trust.

4. **Brand Identity and Consistency**

   Clear communication contributes significantly to establishing and maintaining a consistent brand identity. A company's brand is primarily defined by how it communicates with its external audience. Consistent, clear messaging reinforces the brand's values, propositions, and differentiators in the minds of consumers. For instance, if a company's marketing communications are consistently clear and aligned with its branding, it strengthens customer recognition and loyalty. In contrast, inconsistent or unclear messages can confuse or alienate customers.

5. **Legal and Ethical Responsibility**

   Businesses also have a legal and ethical responsibility to communicate clearly. Miscommunication can lead to breaches of compliance, misunderstandings in contractual obligations, and other legal repercussions. For instance, a poorly drafted contract can lead to disputes and litigation, financially damaging and harming its reputation. Clear, unambiguous communication ensures that all parties understand their rights, duties, and limitations, thereby minimizing the risk of legal complications.

6. Employee Engagement and Morale

Internally, clear communication significantly affects employee engagement and morale. Employees who clearly understand their tasks, the company's goals, and their contribution to the organization's success are more likely to feel valued and motivated. This clarity starts with clear communication from the top down. Regular, clear communication about company performance, changes, and successes makes employees feel included and valued, boosting their motivation and commitment to the company.

§

As any seasoned business writer would attest, the clarity of message in business communication is not just about being understood; it's about being practical, trustworthy, and strategic. It influences every aspect of business operations—from internal management and customer relationships to strategic planning and brand positioning. In the complex web of business interactions, clarity acts as a beacon guiding all parties toward collective success.

POSITIONING

In the competitive business world, positioning is not some frivolous marketing ploy; it's an essential strategy that steers the course of a company's success. From my extensive experience analyzing strategies across various sectors, I can attest to the significant impact effective positioning has on a company's capability to excel, whether the economic climate is booming or facing headwinds. For instance, I positioned myself as a cosmetic dermatologist with the statement, "Where Education Matters and Quality Counts."

The Crux of Strategic Positioning

Positioning involves molding you and your company's identity in the minds of its target market. It's about tailoring your product or service to align with your customer's desires, preferences, and values. Effective positioning distinguishes your brand from the competition by emphasizing unique attributes that matter to customers. When executed well, it creates a distinct niche, setting your brand apart in a crowded marketplace.

Securing Market Relevance

The chief aim of positioning is to carve out relevance. In today's saturated market, consumers can easily get overwhelmed with choices. Effective positioning enables a business to distinctively stand out by defining how its offerings meet the evolving needs of potential customers. This relevance is dynamic; it shifts as consumer preferences and market dynamics evolve. Businesses must continuously refine their positioning to keep pace with these changes, ensuring ongoing relevance.

Crafting a Competitive Edge

A robust positioning strategy is instrumental in building a competitive edge and positioning steers clear of the pitfalls of commoditization by distinctly stating what makes a company unique. When products or services appear interchangeable, price becomes the main distinguishing factor. Clever positioning, however, accentuates unique attributes, benefits, or experiences that competitors can't easily replicate.

Shaping Customer Perceptions

Positioning influences how customers perceive a brand, significantly affecting their purchasing decisions. A company might have superior services or products or offer more value, but without effective positioning, its market potential remains untapped. Thus, positioning must be strategic and intentional, ensuring every customer interaction reinforces the desired brand image and message.

Guiding Business Strategy

Positioning extends its influence beyond mere marketing; it shapes the entire business strategy. It informs product development, customer service, pricing, and distribution strategies. A solid market position guides decision-making and strategic choices, aligning all business aspects with the overarching brand promise.

Encouraging Brand Loyalty and Advocacy

Effective positioning cultivates brand loyalty by consistently meeting or surpassing the expectations established through marketing messages. Customers who perceive that a brand delivers on its promises will likely become repeat buyers and enthusiastic advocates. Brand loyalty lowers sales and marketing costs, as retaining existing customers is typically cheaper than acquiring new ones.

Navigating Market Shifts

Positioning acts like a compass in fluctuating markets, helping businesses navigate changes. It provides a framework to innovate and respond to new challenges without losing their core identity. For example, a company known for innovation can introduce cutting-edge technologies or disrupt existing paradigms, maintaining relevance as market conditions shift.

Boosting Financial Outcomes

Ultimately, effective positioning boosts financial performance. Companies with clear, compelling positions often enjoy higher profit margins, excellent customer retention, and increased market share. They can command premium pricing due to their differentiated offerings and attract more investment because their unique market position stands out.

Unique Selling or Educational Proposition (UEP/ USP)

A Unique Selling Proposition differentiates you from all other competitors - it sets you apart. It emphasizes your uniqueness.

The example I would like to share is that of Tom Monaghan and Domino's Pizza. Tom and his brother bought a rundown pizza store near a university. His brother soon became disillusioned and was bought out by Tom for the price of his broken-down Volkswagen Beatle.

When Tom developed his USP, everything in the highly competitive pizza world changed. It didn't say anything about using tomatoes harvested from the sun-kissed fields of Mt. Olympus. It didn't brag about the crust with its secret formula of dough made from yeast and rising for 24 hours. It didn't even mention "good pizza." It simply said, "Delivered in 30 minutes, or your money refunded." That's it. Tom sold Domino's pizza for billions of dollars in 1998.

The IOFP helps members with their UEP/USP.

Positioning is more than just current status; it's about aiming for where you want to be in your customers' perceptions and the broader market. It's a strategic tool that can determine a company's fortunes when used with skill and foresight. As businesses navigate through the complexities of the global market, the capability to position effectively is not merely an advantage—it's essential.

§

Understanding and mastering the art of positioning is critical—it defines the battlefield where companies vie for supremacy. It is the initial and most crucial step in a series of marketing decisions that dictate a company's destiny. Even the finest products might flounder without precise, compelling positioning, and the most robust enterprises might fade into obscurity. For those aiming to make a lasting impact on the business landscape, mastering positioning is not just important—it's imperative. The IOFP is there to help you with this.

THE BIGGER CAUSE

In business, where pragmatism often reigns, the power of aligning with a larger cause can sometimes be overlooked. However, modern enterprises increasingly recognize that associating with a bigger cause is a moral choice and a strategic imperative. This association, often manifested through corporate social responsibility (CSR) initiatives, sustainability efforts, or philanthropic endeavors, does more than paint a company in a good light; it propels the business forward, fosters innovation, and builds a more profound connection with consumers.

Strategic Advantage through Differentiation

In today's highly competitive market, differentiation is key to survival and growth. Companies that associate with a more significant cause can set themselves apart from their competitors. Differentiation is not just about superior products or services; it's about embodying values that resonate deeply with consumers. According to various studies, more than half of consumers are willing to pay more for products from brands committed to positive social and environmental impact. By aligning with meaningful causes, businesses can tap into this growing consumer base that prioritizes ethical considerations in purchasing decisions.

Enhanced Brand Loyalty and Reputation

When a company commits to a bigger cause, it often sees a direct impact on its brand loyalty. Customers are more likely to return to brands that serve their needs and reflect their values. This loyalty is strengthened when consumers see consistent and genuine commitment rather than one-off charity drives or superficial campaigns. Moreover, in the age of social media, where a company's action can be scrutinized instantly, a sustained commitment to a cause can protect and enhance its reputation, turning potential crises into opportunities to demonstrate corporate values in action.

Attracting and Retaining Talent

Today's workforce, particularly among millennials and Gen Z, seeks more than just employment; they are increasingly driven by purpose and seek out workplaces that reflect their own values. By associating with a larger cause, companies can attract top talent who are skilled and passionately committed to their roles, knowing their work contributes to the greater good. This alignment can reduce turnover rates, increase employee satisfaction, and drive-up productivity as employees feel more connected and engaged with their employer's mission.

Innovation and Longevity

Associating with a bigger cause pushes companies to innovate, as they are forced to solve complex, meaningful problems. This might involve developing new, more sustainable production methods, adopting greener technologies, or finding efficient ways to give back to the community. Such innovations can lead to discoveries that refine a company's offerings, creating entirely new markets or product lines. Furthermore, companies are more likely to think long-term in their strategic planning by focusing on long-term challenges, paving the way for sustainability and longevity in an ever-evolving market landscape.

Building Community and Stakeholder Trust

Businesses are integral to the communities they serve. By associating with a bigger cause, a company demonstrates its commitment to the well-being of its community, which can build immense goodwill and trust among stakeholders. This trust is crucial during times of crisis when the community's support can significantly impact a company's ability to navigate adversity.

Regulatory and Government Favor

Governments and regulatory bodies worldwide are increasingly imposing regulations that favor socially and environmentally responsible companies. By taking the lead in these areas, businesses can ensure compliance and potentially benefit from government incentives like tax breaks, grants, and other supports. Moreover, companies recognized for their corporate social responsibility (CSR) often influence industry standards and regulations, positioning themselves as pioneers in new, regulated markets.

§

Associating with a bigger cause is more than a marketing strategy; it's a strategic asset that can propel a business to new heights of success and relevance. It aligns with the shifting global expectations of corporate conduct and responds to the growing consumer demand for brands with a conscience. In this new business era, the most successful companies will be those that act as forces for good, integrating their profit motives with the broader social and environmental contexts in which they operate. This is not just good ethics; it's a sound business strategy.

The IOFP aligns with bigger causes by charitable giving. Here are just a few causes we help

1. **Our Scholarship Plan** - Every year, several potential members for the IOFP are suggested but cannot afford the fees. So, we've created a scholarship program that allows them to join.

2. **Rotary International Fund** - Rotary helps 1,000's of projects arrows the world. From 1905 to present, very few organizations give the depth and breadth Rotary does. That's why we support Rotary.

3. **#notinmycity** - Every year, hundreds, if not thousands, of children are dragged into childhood prostitution. That's why we partnered with this organization to end it.

4. **Ronald McDonalds House** - RMH alleviates the emotional , financial and physical burden of families with sick and injured children.

5. **Victims of Domestic Violence** - every year, the IOFP parents with organizations to help victims fleeing domestic violence

WRITING THE BOOK

Authorship has unparalleled power in establishing authority and credibility in any field. Writing a book is not just an exercise in self-expression but a strategic move that can elevate a professional to new heights of respect and influence. Here's how Kennedy might argue that writing books is crucial for establishing authority.

Establishing Credibility Through Expertise

Writing a book is arguably the most potent method to demonstrate expertise. In the noisy marketplace of ideas, where opinions and advice are freely offered and often contradictory, a book is a substantial and tangible demonstration of knowledge and dedication to a subject. Unlike shorter content forms, a book allows for deep exploration of concepts, substantiated arguments, and narratives, positioning the author as a committed expert.

Leveraging Perceived Value

A book inherently carries more perceived value than articles, blog posts, or social media content. A book requires a more significant investment of time and effort from both the writer and the reader. For the writer, this investment involves research, organization of thoughts, and often years of experience distilled into pages. For readers, spending hours with a book reflects trust in the author's knowledge and the expectation of gaining substantial benefits, such as new insights or skills.

Longevity and Reach

Books possess a longevity that digital content often lacks. While blog posts and videos might fade into the digital ether, a well-written book can be read and recommended for years, if not decades. This staying power extends an author's reach across time and geography. Kennedy often points out how his books have helped him reach audiences he could never have interacted with directly, continuing to influence long after their publication.

Marketing and Speaking Opportunities

Authors are frequently invited to speak at conferences, appear on panels, and give interviews. These opportunities provide additional exposure and act as endorsements of the author's authority and thought leadership. Kennedy argues that a book acts like a multi-purpose marketing tool functioning as a calling card, portfolio piece, and sales brochure all rolled into one long after other marketing efforts have been exhausted.

Networking and Professional Opportunities

Writing a book can open doors to new professional connections and opportunities. Other experts, influencers, and decision-makers often seek out authors for collaborations, consulting, or business ventures. Kennedy has recounted numerous instances where deals and partnerships were initiated by someone impressed with his books. The credibility of being a published author can be a powerful catalyst for new business and professional growth.

Personal Brand Development

Personal brand is everything. Writing a book significantly builds a personal brand by differentiating an author from competitors, showcasing unique perspectives, and creating a narrative around personal and professional identity. A book can be a cornerstone of a personal brand, encapsulating the author's philosophy, approach, and expertise in a form that is easily accessible and sharable.

Passive Income

Books can generate passive income while not being the primary focus for authority building. Once written, a book can sell indefinitely, providing a continuous source of revenue without ongoing effort. This financial benefit is not insignificant, though secondary to the authority and opportunities a book generates.

Writing a book is much more than just putting words on paper; it's a strategic endeavor that can elevate one's professional stature, open new avenues of opportunity, and create lasting personal and professional impacts. As Kennedy would put it, a book is not just a product but a profound statement of authority and expertise that resonates with audiences and establishes a lasting legacy in one's field.

I have written seventeen books when I was a cosmetic doctor, and since retiring - have written three more International best-sellers.

- Secrets to Living A Fantastic Life
- Pillars of Success
- bLU volume 1

"Everything I've learned I've learned in books"

~. Books with Joe Vitale, Ken Honda, Dr. Allen Steven Lycka

Unsure of your ability to produce a book? No problem. We have an experienced team to help make you a bestseller.

SHAMELESS SELF-PROMOTION

Dan S. Kennedy, my mentor, espouses the virtues of vigorous, unapologetic self-promotion. His philosophy is that being "shameless" about marketing oneself or one's business isn't just beneficial—it's necessary for survival and success in today's competitive marketplace. Channeling Kennedy's candid, no-nonsense style has helped me succeed in my life and can help you.

Understanding the Value of Visibility

One thing needs to be highlighted - obscurity is a far greater threat to any business or professional than overexposure. Modesty is a luxury you cannot afford if you aim to be profitable. From this perspective, "Shameless self-promotion" isn't about being obnoxious or unethical; it's about maximizing visibility and asserting your market presence. "If they can't see you, they can't buy from you," The first step to being seen is to put yourself out there unabashedly.

Crafting a Magnetic Personal Brand

Creating a compelling personal brand helps overcome obscurity. This brand must be distinctive, memorable, and reflect one's unique value proposition. Your brand is not just what you sell or what you do but the story you tell and the emotions you evoke. Define your brand boldly and clearly, ensure it resonates with your target audience, and promote it relentlessly. "Be the brand," I urge. Personal and business brands should be so intertwined that they become indistinguishable.

Utilizing Every Platform Available

Leverage every available platform for promotion—from traditional media like direct mail and print advertising to digital arenas such as social media and email marketing. Each platform has unique advantages and could be used to reach different audience segments. Your mantra should be to "be everywhere your customers are" and use each platform's strengths to your advantage, ensuring consistent messaging that reinforces your brand identity.

The Power of Direct Response Marketing

Recognize the power of direct response marketing—creating advertising that calls for an immediate response, such as a call to action that leads to a purchase or a sign-up. Remember the importance of making every piece of marketing material count towards measurable, actionable outcomes. Focus on clear, compelling copywriting that directly speaks to the needs and desires of the target audience, urging them to act now rather than later.

Building a Narrative Around Success

Emphasize the importance of storytelling in marketing. Building a narrative around success stories, customer testimonials, and personal anecdotes that showcase the effectiveness of your product or service. This approach humanizes the brand and provides social proof, essential in persuading new customers to buy into your offer.

Educational Marketing as a Tool for Promotion

Educational marketing is another crucial aspect that involves using valuable content to educate your audience about your industry, service, or product while subtly promoting your brand. He'd argue that by offering real value through information and insights, you position yourself as an authority in your field, naturally attracting more clients or customers. This can be achieved by regularly publishing articles, blogs, books, speeches, and seminars as educational marketing methods.

Networking and Strategic Alliances

Remember the power of networks and strategic alliances. Cultivate relationships with other professionals and businesses for mutual benefits. Strategic alliances and joint ventures can extend your reach and tap into new customer bases. Approach these opportunities pragmatically, creating win-win scenarios that enhance visibility and market presence.

Unyielding Persistence and Consistency

Persistence and consistency are vital in self-promotion. He often speaks about the "drip-drip-drip" approach—maintaining a steady, ongoing presence in your customers' lives. This could be through regular emails, constant social media updates, or recurrent advertising campaigns. The key is continuously engaging your audience, reminding them of your existence and value proposition.

In summary, "shameless self-promotion" encapsulates a robust, assertive approach to marketing that refuses to shy away from the spotlight. Self-promotion is not just a tactic but a necessary endeavor for achieving and sustaining business success. His message is clear: embrace visibility, articulate your value boldly, and never apologize for advocating passionately for your business.

As a cosmetic doctor, I wrote a monthly newsletter featuring my dog, Peppe, who became a star. He'd tell stories about me that I could Never tell and became famous in the process. People could run home on the day the newsletter arrived just to read Peppe's chronicles.

THE NEWS MEDIA

Effective news media use is crucial for successful public relations strategies in today's rapidly evolving media landscape. As publicists, our role transcends merely beyond disseminating information; it involves crafting compelling narratives, building relationships, and navigating the complexities of various media channels to enhance our client's public image and achieve strategic objectives.

Crafting Compelling Narratives

At the heart of effective media use is the ability to craft compelling narratives. A narrative that resonates with both the media and the public can significantly amplify your message's impact. This involves presenting facts and weaving them into a story that aligns with your audience's values and interests. This requires profoundly understanding your target demographic and anticipating how they receive and interpret information.

To create these narratives, start with the core message you want to convey. Consider the emotional pull of your story—is it inspiring, alarming, or reassuring? Next, build a newsworthy and relevant storyline, strategically timing it to fit current discussions and sentiments.

Building Media Relationships

One must emphasize the importance of building and maintaining robust relationships with the media. These relationships are the conduits through which narratives flow into the public domain since they aren't merely transactional interactions but opportunities to create mutual benefit and trust.

Fostering strong media relationships involves consistent engagement and providing value to journalists and editors by understanding their beats, burdens, deadlines, and story interests. Be ready to serve as a reliable, accurate, timely, and relevant source of information to become a go-to person for journalists. This trust is invaluable and can significantly influence your ability to place stories effectively.

Leveraging Multiple Media Channels

In the digital age, publicists must manage various media channels. Traditional media—newspapers, television, and radio— are still powerful, but digital platforms, such as social media, blogs, and podcasts, offer more targeted outreach capabilities and audience interaction.

Each channel has its unique strengths and audience demographics. Television might be an excellent tool for reaching a broad audience, but Twitter or Instagram can be more effective for quick, impactful engagements with younger demographics. Therefore, a successful media strategy involves choosing the right channel and tailoring the message to fit the medium while maintaining a cohesive brand voice across all platforms.

Monitoring and Adapting to Media Trends

The media environment is dynamic, with constant trends and technological advancements. Practical media usage requires staying ahead of these trends and adapting strategies accordingly. This could mean exploring emerging social platforms, adapting to new content formats like short videos or podcasts, or employing analytics tools to gain deeper insights into audience behavior.

Monitoring media outcomes through analytics enables publicists to understand what works and what doesn't, refining real-time strategies to optimize outcomes. This data-driven approach ensures that efforts are focused and messages resonate with the intended audience.

Crisis Management

Finally, effective news media use also involves being prepared for crisis management. In times of crisis, the speed and accuracy of your response can make or break your client's reputation. Having a crisis communication plan, knowing who your allies are in the media, and how to use the news cycles to your advantage are all critical in managing negative situations.

Preparation involves:

• Training and drills.

• Crafting potential response scenarios.

• Establishing clear communication channels internally and with the media.

When a crisis strikes, using these preparations to control the narrative can significantly mitigate potential damage to your client's public image.

§

Mastering news media in public relations is both an art and a science. It combines creative narrative construction, strategic media engagement, agility in adapting to new trends, and meticulous execution. For those managing public images, seeing a well-crafted message positively impact its audience is immensely rewarding. Effective media use enhances our clients' stature and fortifies their relationship with the public, ensuring sustained success in their various endeavors.

SERVICE: THE COMPETITIVE EDGE

In industries where products and prices are often similar, service can be the critical differentiator. Customers often choose providers based on the expected quality of service, underscoring its value as a competitive advantage. According to a study by American Express, more than half of Americans have scrapped a planned purchase or transaction because of bad service. Thus, excellent service not only retains customers but also prevents potential losses.

Building Brand Loyalty

Service drives brand loyalty. Consumers who receive high-quality service are more likely to remain loyal to the brand, even in the face of competitors' attempts to lure them away with lower prices or more attractive offerings. The White House Office of Consumer Affairs reports that acquiring a new customer is 6-7 times more expensive than retaining an existing one. Loyal customers contribute through repeat purchases and often become brand advocates, generating valuable word-of-mouth marketing.

Enhancing Brand Reputation

In the digital age, a company's reputation is significantly influenced by its service. Social media platforms and review sites amplify customers' voices, and a single negative service experience can spread quickly, potentially causing significant reputational damage. Conversely, positive service experiences can enhance a brand's reputation. Outstanding service leads to positive reviews and testimonials that enhance the company's image and attract new customers.

Driving Business Growth

High-quality service contributes directly to business growth. Satisfied customers tend to spend more and purchase more frequently. Furthermore, by exceeding customer expectations, companies can charge a premium for their products and services as people are willing to pay more for superior service. According to a study by PwC, 73% of people consider customer experience to be an important factor in their purchasing decisions, just behind price and product quality.

Fostering a Culture of Improvement

Prioritizing service also fosters a culture of continuous improvement within the organization. When service is integral to a company's operations, customer feedback is continuously sought and valued, which drives ongoing enhancements to products, services, and processes. This proactive approach ensures the company meets and anticipates customer needs.

Strategic Implications of Service

On a strategic level, focusing on service aligns the organization towards customer-centricity, integrating marketing, sales, operations, and logistics efforts to add value to every customer interaction. This holistic approach maximizes the efficiency of resource allocation and improves the effectiveness of operational processes.

Challenges in Implementing Service Excellence

Achieving service excellence is not without challenges. A well-trained, empowered, and motivated workforce must consistently deliver high-quality service. It also involves the implementation of robust systems and processes that can support the delivery of this service. Moreover, a culture that prioritizes service must be actively nurtured and maintained, often requiring a shift in mindset at all levels of the organization.

§

In today's business landscape, service is crucial as products become more commoditized and global competition intensifies. Companies that leverage service as a strategic advantage not only enhance their competitive edge but also set themselves up for sustained success.

Thus, for businesses looking to survive and thrive, focusing on service is not merely an option but an imperative. It requires commitment, strategic planning, and a culture that supports and rewards service excellence. The payoff, however, is a more loyal customer base, a stronger brand, and, ultimately, a more successful business.

CELEBRITIES

Celebrity endorsements and associations have long been a cornerstone in companies' marketing and branding strategies for decades. Their importance lies in the unique blend of visibility, credibility, and appeal they bring to a brand, profoundly influencing consumer perceptions and behaviors.

At its core, celebrity association leverages the fame and popularity of an individual to boost a brand's image and sales. This relationship between celebrity and company is symbiotic: the brand gains the celebrity's attention and glamour; in return, the celebrity secures financial benefits and enhances the brand.

Visibility

Celebrities naturally command attention. By associating with them, brands can cut through the noise of a crowded marketplace. This visibility is especially critical in today's digital age, where consumers are bombarded with endless streams of content. Therefore, celebrities can help a brand stand out, drawing immediate attention and fostering quicker brand recognition.

Credibility and Trust

When a respected celebrity endorses a product, they lend credibility to it. Consumers often perceive celebrity-endorsed products as more reliable or of higher quality because someone they admire, or trust has approved them. This reduces the perceived risk of trying a new product, which can significantly shorten the consumer's decision-making process.

Emotional Connection

Since celebrities often hold a special place in the hearts of fans, brands can harness this emotional connection to create deeper, more meaningful relationships with consumers. When a favorite celebrity uses or recommends a product, fans are more likely to feel a personal connection to the brand. This can lead to stronger brand loyalty and advocacy, as consumers indirectly relate their product use with support or connection to their admired celebrity.

Influence and Trendsetting

Celebrities are often trendsetters whose choices and behaviors, including their brand preferences, are closely watched and often emulated by fans. When a celebrity is seen with a particular product, it can quickly become a must-have item. This trendsetting capability makes them powerful allies for brands looking to establish or increase the market viability of their products.

Strategic Considerations

Despite the apparent benefits, celebrity associations are not without risks and require strategic consideration to maximize their effectiveness.

Relevance

The celebrity must resonate with the target audience and align with the brand's identity and customer demographics. A mismatch can lead to a lack of connection or, worse, backlash if the celebrity's behavior conflicts with the brand's values or the expectations of its customers.

Overexposure

Overreliance on celebrities can also be risky. If a celebrity endorses multiple brands, their endorsement might lose its impact. Overexposure can dilute the association's uniqueness and reduce the celebrity endorsement's effectiveness for any brand.

Longevity and Consistency

Long-term associations are typically more effective than short-term endorsements, building a consistent story and trust around the brand. However, brands must be ready to manage the risks of a long-term commitment, including any potential negative publicity involving the celebrity.

§

Celebrity association can be a potent tool for brands, offering a unique combination of visibility, credibility, and emotional appeal that can significantly influence consumer behavior. However, celebrity endorsements must be approached with careful planning and strategic foresight, like any marketing strategy. Brands must choose the right celebrity, craft the right message, and manage the association thoughtfully to harness its full potential while mitigating associated risks.

AWARDS

Winning awards in the business world is more than just an individual achievement: it is a strategic asset that can catalyze long-term success for both professionals and their organizations. It is a topic that merits thoughtful consideration, especially in a competitive landscape where differentiation is key to standing out. Here, we explore why receiving accolades is crucial in various facets of the business domain.

1. **Enhancement of Brand Reputation**

   Awards serve as a third-party endorsement of a company's commitment to excellence. When a reputable institution recognizes a business, it affirms the company's competencies in the eyes of industry peers and elevates its standing among consumers. This enhanced perception boosts credibility, a vital asset in attracting new customers and retaining existing ones. The recognition that comes with awards can transform a brand's identity from one among many to a leader in its field.

2. **Employee Motivation and Attraction**

   Awards boost employee morale by acknowledging hard work and dedication, enhancing job satisfaction and loyalty. Moreover, being part of an award-winning team can make employees proud to be associated with their employer, fostering a positive workplace culture. From a recruitment perspective, awards make a company more attractive to top talent as prospective employees are often drawn to organizations celebrated for their excellence for better career opportunities and growth.

3. **Market Differentiation**

   In saturated markets, standing out from the competition can be challenging. Awards provide a clear differentiation point, signaling to customers, investors, and partners that the company is a leader in its field. This differentiation is especially crucial for businesses in industries where products and services are largely homogeneous. Winning awards can be a deciding factor for consumers choosing between similar options, as it highlights superior quality or service.

4. **Investor Confidence**

   Awards can enhance a company's appeal to investors. They serve as a proxy for company health and prospects, indicating that the business is performing well and can achieve excellence. It is particularly valuable for startups or companies seeking further investment, as awards increase visibility in a crowded marketplace and make a business more attractive for investment proposition.

5. **Marketing and PR Opportunities**

   Winning an award provides substantial marketing and public relations opportunities, allowing a company to promote itself as an award-winning brand, which can be a powerful addition to marketing campaigns. This type of recognition creates content that can resonate well on social media, press releases, and across communication channels, enhancing overall brand visibility. Furthermore, it offers a unique angle for storytelling in marketing communications, focusing on proven excellence and industry leadership.

6. **Customer Trust and Loyalty**

   Awards build customer trust, making businesses appear more reliable and committed to quality. This perception influences buying decisions and can increase customer retention rates. In the long term, this trust translates into greater customer loyalty, as consumers tend to stick with brands recognized for their superior offerings.

7. **Encouragement of Internal Quality and Innovation**

   The process of applying for and winning awards can foster a culture of improvement and innovation within a company. It encourages a business to look critically at its operations, identify areas for improvement, and innovate to meet or exceed industry standards. This internal drive for excellence can lead to better business practices, higher quality products and services, and improved operational efficiencies.

8. **Networking Opportunities**

   Awards often create networking opportunities with top performers and industry leaders. These interactions can lead to partnerships, mentorships, and exchanges of ideas that can propel a company forward.

§

The importance of winning awards extends beyond the trophy on the shelf. It impacts various aspects of a business, from brand perception and employee morale to market differentiation and investor confidence. In essence, awards are not just recognitions of past achievements but also a forward-looking catalyst for future success. Thus, in the strategic playbook of any ambitious company, aiming for and achieving award-winning excellence can reap dividends across all fronts of the business spectrum.

SPEECHES

Speeches are a fundamental element of leadership and communication in the business, playing a crucial role in shaping perceptions, influencing opinions, and motivating change. The ability to deliver compelling speeches is a powerful tool for executives, managers, and entrepreneurs alike. This article explores the multifaceted importance of speeches in business, examining how they function as vehicles for leadership, catalysts for transformation, and instruments of corporate strategy.

1. **Leadership and Vision Communication**

   Speeches are key to articulating a company's vision to stakeholders, including employees, investors, customers, and partners. The power of a well-delivered speech lies in its ability to clarify the company's future direction and inspire listeners to envision their roles within this future framework. Leaders like Steve Jobs and Elon Musk have famously used product launch speeches to introduce new products and convey larger visions of change and innovation that align their teams and excite their customer base.

2. **Influence and Persuasion**

   Speeches are powerful tools of influence and persuasion, crafted to sway opinions and encourage action. Whether it's convincing investors to back a new project, persuading partners to join an initiative, or motivating employees to adopt a new business strategy, speeches can effectively marshal arguments and emotional appeals to achieve desired outcomes. Persuasive speaking involves connecting emotionally with the audience, making them feel invested in the presented narrative.

3. **Motivation and Employee Engagement**

   Speeches can significantly impact employee motivation and engagement. A stirring address by a leader can rejuvenate teams and renew their commitment to company goals, particularly during crucial times of change or challenge, such as during mergers, acquisitions, or major market shifts. Such speeches can transform uncertainty and fear into determination and loyalty, aligning the workforce with a commitment to overcome obstacles and reach new heights.

4. **Corporate Identity and Culture Shaping**

   Leaders use speeches to mold and reinforce corporate identity and culture. The themes, stories, and values highlighted in speeches define what a company stands for and how it differentiates itself from competitors. Over time, these elements become woven into the fabric of the company's culture, influencing everything from day-to-day operations to strategic decisions. Speeches can serve as a reminder of these values, reinforcing the behaviors that reflect the company's ethos and aspirations.

5. **Crisis Management and Public Relations**

   In times of crisis, speeches are critical for managing public relations and restoring stakeholder confidence. A well-crafted speech can address concerns, acknowledge mistakes, and outline a clear path forward, thus mitigating damage to the company's reputation. A speech's immediate and personal nature allows a leader to express sincerity and resolve, helping to rebuild trust and reassure stakeholders that the company is capable of navigating through turbulent times.

6. **Networking and Industry Positioning**

   Speeches also provide a platform for networking and establishing thought leadership within an industry. By speaking at conferences, seminars, and workshops, business leaders can share insights, forecast trends, and position themselves and their companies as influential voices in their fields, leading to new business opportunities and collaborations.

7. **Feedback and Engagement Loop**

   Engaging with an audience through speeches creates a feedback loop invaluable for business strategy and development. Audience reactions and interactions can provide immediate insights into the market's response to new ideas or initiatives, allowing companies to adjust their strategies in real-time. This dynamic aspect of speeches makes them essential for testing ideas and gauging stakeholder reactions in a relatively low-risk environment.

8. **Training and Development**

   Finally, speeches play an educational role in training and developing employees. Leaders can use speeches to introduce new strategies, technologies, or methodologies, providing large groups of employees with consistent training simultaneously. This function is crucial in ensuring all team members have the knowledge and skills necessary to execute their roles effectively.

§

Speeches in business are strategic tools for leadership, influence, motivation, and more. They are essential for articulating the vision, driving change, shaping corporate culture, managing crises, and establishing industry leadership. As such, mastering the art of speechmaking is a critical skill for any business leader committed to achieving and sustaining success in the competitive world of modern business.

BIG THINGS

Few subjects evoke as much excitement and anxiety as tackling "big things"—projects or ambitions that go beyond everyday tasks. The allure of taking on monumental challenges can be irresistible, yet the road to accomplishing them is often fraught with hurdles that can deter even the most ambitious entrepreneurs. From my experience with large-scale projects, I can attest that the journey is as important as the destination.

Why Work on Big Things?

First, let's define what it means to work on "big things." These aren't just large tasks but projects or goals that stretch your capabilities and require substantial resources with the potential to influence your market or the world significantly. They are the types of endeavors that can define your career.

There are numerous reasons for taking on such colossal tasks. For one, they push you out of your comfort zone, forcing you to innovate and think differently. They also set you apart from the competition, as few possess the courage and drive to tackle such beasts. Moreover, big projects can lead to substantial financial rewards and strategic advantages.

The Psychology of Big Endeavors

Understanding the psychological underpinnings of embarking on significant projects is crucial. Fear of failure is a common barrier. The bigger the project, the more daunting it can seem. However, as I often emphasize in my writings and seminars, the mindset with which you approach a challenge often determines your outcome. It would be best to cultivate a mindset of resilience, clarity, and unwavering focus.

To work on big things successfully, you also need a deep-seated belief in the project's value. This belief fuels the persistence required when inevitable obstacles arise. Every major project will test your resolve; without a strong conviction, you might falter when you most need to persevere.

Strategic Planning and Execution

No amount of motivation can substitute for meticulous planning and execution. The adage "fail to plan, plan to fail" holds particularly true in large-scale endeavors. Start by breaking down the project into manageable parts, which makes the overall task less intimidating and allows for more detailed planning and assessment.

Resource allocation is another critical consideration. Big projects often require significant resources, including time, money, and manpower. One of the entrepreneurs' biggest mistakes is underestimating these resources, leading to overextension and failure. Therefore, realistic appraisal and management of resources are paramount.

Risk Management

Working on big things inherently involves higher risks, which requires understanding for mitigation rather than avoidance. This consists of conducting thorough market research, scenario planning, and continuous monitoring of project variables. In addition, contingency plans should always be in place. The ability to pivot and adapt strategies is indispensable in managing large projects.

Leveraging the Right Team

No man is an island, especially when tackling monumental tasks. The importance of assembling a capable team cannot be overstated. Each member should not only possess the right skills but also share a commitment to the project's goals. As a leader, you will keep the team motivated and focused, ensuring that each member's efforts align with the project's objectives.

Sustaining Momentum

Maintaining momentum in long-term projects is challenging. Interest can wane, and the initial excitement can dissipate, requiring setting short-term goals and celebrating milestones. These provide continuous motivation and a sense of achievement. Additionally, regularly revisiting the project's vision can rejuvenate enthusiasm and focus.

§

In conclusion, working on big things is not for the faint-hearted. It demands a confluence of courage, meticulous planning, and robust execution. It also requires an understanding of the psychological and strategic nuances involved. However, the rewards can be substantial, not just in financial gain but also in personal growth and the satisfaction of achieving something truly impactful.

As you embark on your next big project, remember these principles. With the right mindset, strategy, and team, you can tackle anything—no matter the size. Remember, the winners think big and act boldly in a world of high stakes and big challenges.

In today's rapidly evolving marketplace, the concept of service has transcended mere customer interactions to become a foundational element of successful business strategy. More than just a department or a function, service is the very ethos that can set a company apart in a crowded field. Service excellence cultivates customer loyalty, enhances the brand reputation, drives business growth, and fosters a culture of continuous improvement. For businesses aiming to rise above the competition, prioritizing high-quality service is not just important—it's essential.

THE TEAM

Building a great team is fundamental to business success, much like laying the cornerstone of a strong edifice. The task requires a keen understanding of people, a vision for the future, and the ability to foster an environment where diverse talents can synergize effectively. Below, I've distilled the essence of building a great team by blending timeless principles and contemporary insights.

Vision and Purpose

A great team starts with a clear and compelling vision. This vision serves as the North Star, guiding the team's efforts and ensuring alignment with the organization's broader objectives. A leader's primary task is to communicate this vision in an inspiring and clear way. Teams must understand what they are working toward and why it matters. This sense of purpose is crucial for motivation and can significantly enhance engagement and productivity.

Selecting the Right People

Jim Collins famously advised in "Good to Great" to get the right people on the bus (and the wrong people off the bus) before figuring out where to drive it. When building a team, look beyond skills and experience; consider how potential team members align with the company's culture and values. Diversity in thought, background, and expertise can enrich a team's creative potential and problem-solving capacity. However, these differences must be harmonized by a shared commitment to common goals and ethical standards.

Fostering Communication

Effective communication is the lifeblood of any successful team. It's not merely about ensuring regular discussions or frequent meetings. Rather, it's about establishing open lines of communication where ideas can be exchanged freely, and feedback is both given and received constructively. As a leader, encourage transparency and facilitate a safe environment where every voice can be heard without fear of judgment or reprisal.

Building Trust

Trust is foundational to any high-functioning team. It allows for the open exchange of ideas, reduces the need for cumbersome checks and balances, and speeds up decision-making. Building trust takes time and requires consistency, integrity, and authenticity. Leaders must model these behaviors and ensure that ethical conduct and reliability are expected from everyone. Regular team-building activities and social interactions outside work can strengthen bonds and foster trust.

Empowering Team Members

Empowerment is key to unlocking a team's full potential. This means providing team members with the resources, authority, and autonomy to make decisions within their areas of responsibility. Empowerment boosts morale and drives engagement by showing team members that their contributions are valued and that they play an essential role in the team's success. It also requires them to be accountable for their decisions and learn from successes and failures.

Adapting to Change

Flexibility and adaptability are crucial traits for any team in today's fast-paced business environment. Teams must be prepared to pivot quickly in response to new challenges and opportunities. This agility can be facilitated by maintaining a learning orientation within the team, where continuous improvement is the norm, and staying attuned to external shifts in the market and industry.

Recognition and Reward

Recognizing and rewarding team members' efforts is vital in sustaining motivation and encouraging superior performance. Recognition should be timely, specific, and aligned with the team's values and objectives. It doesn't always have to be monetary; often, public acknowledgment of a job well done or the opportunity for career advancement can be equally, if not more, motivating.

Continuous Improvement

Finally, a great team is always a work in progress. An ongoing effort should be made to refine processes, enhance skills, and deepen relationships. Regular feedback loops, where team members can assess their performance and discuss ways to improve, are crucial. This helps address any issues before they become problematic and contributes to a culture of excellence and high performance.

§

In conclusion, building a great team is less about a series of steps and more about cultivating an environment where people can come together to achieve something greater than the sum of their parts. It requires vision, commitment, and a deep understanding of human potential and organizational dynamics. With the right approach, any leader can transform a group of individuals into a powerhouse team that is prepared to face whatever challenges come their way.

SOLUTIONS

Adopting a systematic approach to problem-solving is essential in tackling complex challenges, whether in business, technology, or everyday life. This involves identifying the problem, understanding its root causes, generating potential solutions, evaluating them, and finally implementing the most effective one. Here's a deeper dive into a structured framework that can guide individuals and organizations in solving problems effectively.

1. **Clearly Define the Problem**

    The first step in solving any problem is to define it clearly, as misunderstanding leads to ineffective solutions. A clear problem statement should be concise and focused, describing not only the symptoms but also the impact of the problem. This may involve collecting data, seeking feedback, and observing the problem.

    Example:

    If a business is experiencing declining sales, the problem should be stated as *"Sales have declined by 30% over the last quarter due to decreased customer engagement and increased competition."*

2. **Conduct Thorough Analysis**

    After defining the problem, understand its underlying causes. This usually involves gathering more information and analyzing data. Tools like the 5 Whys, SWOT analysis (Strengths, Weaknesses, Opportunities, Threats), and Root Cause Analysis are helpful here.

    Example:

    For declining sales, a company might perform customer interviews, competitor analysis, and review sales data to pinpoint areas where competitors outperform, or customer needs have evolved.

3. Brainstorm Possible Solutions

With a solid understanding of the problem, the brainstorming phase involves generating a range of solutions without judgment. The key is quantity over quality, as more ideas typically lead to better solutions. Techniques like mind mapping, brainstorming sessions, or creative ideation workshops can facilitate this process.

Example:

To address sales decline, potential solutions could include introducing new products, improving marketing strategies, revising pricing, enhancing customer service, or implementing loyalty programs.

4. Evaluate and Select Solutions

After generating ideas, the next step is to evaluate each solution based on criteria such as feasibility, cost, time, and potential impact. Decision-making tools like cost-benefit analysis, decision matrices, or even pilot testing can be useful.

Example:

The business might find that introducing a new product line is too costly and time-consuming in the short term, but revising the pricing structure and enhancing digital marketing campaigns could be implemented more quickly and cost-effectively.

5. Develop an Implementation Plan

Once a solution is selected, creating a detailed action plan is crucial, outlining the steps to be taken, resources required, timelines, and responsibilities. It's also important to anticipate potential challenges and plan for contingencies.

Example:

To enhance digital marketing campaigns, the plan might include hiring a digital marketing agency, setting up campaign goals, defining key performance indicators (KPIs), and scheduling regular reviews to track progress.

6. **Implement the Solution**

   With the plan in place, proceed with execution. Effective implementation requires managing resources, leading teams, and maintaining clear communication. Monitor progress and adjust as needed to ensure success.

   Example:

   As the new marketing campaigns roll out, the company should monitor metrics such as engagement rates, click-through rates, and ultimately sales figures, adjusting the campaigns according to these metrics.

7. **Evaluate and Learn**

   After implementation, evaluating the outcome against the expected results is crucial. This step determines if the problem has been solved effectively and what lessons can be learned for future problem-solving efforts.

   Example:

   If the revised marketing strategies and pricing adjustments do not yield expected sales improvements, it might be necessary to revisit the analysis phase to check for missed information or additional factors.

8. **Continuous Improvement**

   Problem-solving is an ongoing process. Even after implementing a solution, begin the cycle of continuous improvement. This iterative process ensures that solutions evolve in response to changing conditions and new information.

   Example:

   Regularly scheduled strategy reviews can help the business adapt quickly to new challenges or opportunities in the market.

§

Effective problem-solving requires a structured approach, creativity, and persistence. By following these steps, individuals and organizations can find innovative solutions and turn challenges into opportunities for growth and improvement. Each problem presents a unique set of circumstances and constraints, but the fundamental process of identifying, analyzing, and solving these problems can be universally applied.

NEVER BE BORING

This is the unwritten commandment in business and life

In the ever-evolving circus of business, where attention is the tightrope and your audience the ravenous lions, one commandment stands paramount: Thou shalt not bore. Ignoring this can be as disastrous as a trapeze act foregoing the net. In a world clogged with noise, mediocrity, and the constant drone of the unremarkable, the ability to captivate is not just an asset; it's your lifeline.

First, understand that the marketplace, much like a street in Vegas, is an arena of sensory overload. Here, only the loud, the bright, and the audacious survive. The average consumer is bombarded with up to 10,000 marketing messages daily. If your message is as dull as dishwater, you're not just background noise but practically non-existent.

Let's get something straight: when I say don't be boring, I don't mean you should be a dancing monkey. Being interesting isn't about cheap tricks or obnoxious noise. It's about being ruthlessly effective in engaging your audience's core desires and fears. Everyone has a radio station they tune into: WIIFM (What's in It for Me?). Your job is to broadcast on that frequency loud and clear.

1. **Start with the Story**

   People don't buy goods and services; they buy stories, promises, and the hope of a better tomorrow. The essence of not being boring lies in storytelling. Whether it's the rags-to-riches tale of your startup or the transformational power of your product, you need a narrative that sticks like superglue. A good story is the bridge between anonymity and fame in the marketing world.

   Remember, a great story needs conflict. Without a dragon, there's no hero. Without a villain, there's no victory. What are you fighting against? Mediocrity? Inconvenience? The existential dread of an unfulfilled life? Pinpoint the enemy and show your audience how you swing the sword.

2. **Use the Element of Surprise**

    Predictability is the fast track to oblivion. Surprise your audience—not just once, but continuously. This keeps the adrenaline pumping and the brain engaged. Surprise doesn't mean you should rejig your product line every Tuesday. Instead, it's about how you present your message. Break patterns, defy expectations, and occasionally, throw in a curveball that makes your audience rethink their life choices.

3. **Be Dangerously Specific**

    Generalities are the refuge of the timid. To capture attention, be as sharp as a sniper's bullet. Specificity in your messaging shows you know your audience down to their last whim. It's about going beyond "women aged 20-30" and knowing that you're talking to Jessica, 29, yoga enthusiast and green tea aficionado, who's secretly terrified she won't make it before the biological clock strikes midnight.

4. **Infuse Personality**

    Why do people love Richard Branson, Elon Musk, or any charismatic leader? They have a personality that could either start a party or a fight. Inject your personality into your business. If you're quirky, be gloriously quirky. If you're a nerd, wield your geekdom like a sword. Bland is forgettable. Remember, people might forget what you said, but they'll never forget how you made them feel.

5. **Keep Evolving**

    Stagnation is the first sign of death in any business venture. What worked yesterday might be today's snooze fest. Keep your ear to the ground. Be looking for the next trend, technology, or taco-flavored cheesecake that could revolutionize your industry. Adapt, evolve, and revolve if you must, but never stand still.

6. **Educate Entertainingly**

You've hit gold if you can educate someone about something they need to know while entertaining them. The best marketing feels like learning something cool from a friend over drinks, not like a lecture from the guy who invented watching Paint Dry. Make your audience smarter to engage with you and do it with flair.

In conclusion, never being boring isn't just about having a few tricks up your sleeve. It's a philosophy, a way of life, a relentless pursuit of engagement. It's about ensuring that every touchpoint with your audience—be it an ad, a product, or an email—leaves them a little more intrigued, invested, and interested.

Remember, in the grand marketplace of life, the most unforgivable sin is to be forgettable. So, paint your business in vivid colors, shout your story from the rooftops.

TRIANGLE OF PRE-EMINENCE™

The Synergy of Expertise, Extraordinary Marketing, and Community Service

In the ever-evolving business landscape, success often hinges on more than just the quality of a product or service. It is also shaped by a company's ability to market itself effectively, engage with customers, and contribute to the community.

The synergy between expertise/customer service, extraordinary marketing, and community service forms a powerful triangle that can elevate a business from merely surviving to thriving.

Expertise and Customer Service

Expertise refers to the depth of knowledge and skill in a particular area. This expertise differentiates a business from its competitors and is a critical factor in attracting and retaining customers. However, possessing expertise isn't enough; it must be effectively communicated and utilized through excellent customer service. This means addressing customer needs efficiently, anticipating them, and offering solutions that add value.

For example, a tech company that develops cutting-edge software and provides insightful, responsive support ensures that its customers make the most of its products. This expertise-driven customer service builds a reputation for reliability and quality, encouraging customer loyalty and fostering a positive brand image.

Extraordinary Marketing

Marketing is how a business communicates its expertise and values to the world. Extraordinary marketing goes beyond traditional advertising; it involves deeply understanding customer needs, desires, and behavior patterns. This can include everything from data-driven digital marketing strategies to creative content marketing and more.

An extraordinary marketing campaign leverages various channels and technologies to reach and resonate with its target audience, creating memorable experiences. Apple, for instance, excels in this area by marketing its products not just as electronics but as essential tools for creativity and productivity, wrapped in a sleek, user-friendly design.

Community Service

Community service is often overlooked in business strategies, but it plays a crucial role in building trust and goodwill within the local community. Engaging in community service helps a company demonstrate its values and commitment to social responsibility, strengthening its brand and appeal to a broader customer base.

Businesses that invest in their communities through charitable donations, volunteering, or sponsoring local events often enhance their public image and create new networking opportunities. Moreover, community service can boost employee morale and attract talent who value social responsibility.

Synergistic Impact

When these three elements—expertise and customer service, extraordinary marketing, and community service—work together, they create a synergy that can significantly boost a company's success. Each component reinforces the others; for example, a company known for its expert and customer-centric service will find it easier to craft compelling marketing narratives. Similarly, a business that actively participates in community service can leverage those stories in its marketing to highlight its values and differentiate itself from competitors.

Real-World Application

Consider a local bakery that specializes in organic, handcrafted bread. The bakery's expertise in making high-quality bread is a core part of its business. By training staff to provide knowledgeable and friendly service, the bakery enhances customer interactions, ensuring customers feel valued and well-served.

To market itself, the bakery might use social media to share engaging content about the benefits of organic ingredients and the artisanal methods used. Such an approach draws in customers who value health and craftsmanship. Additionally, suppose the bakery supports local farmers or food banks. In that case, it not only gives back to the community but also strengthens its marketing message about commitment to quality and community welfare.

§

The triangle of expertise/customer service, extraordinary marketing, and community service is more than just a theoretical concept; it's a practical strategy for building a robust, sustainable business. By excelling in these areas, a company can enhance its reputation, deepen customer loyalty, and contribute positively to its community- all of which are essential to long-term success. This approach benefits the business and its stakeholders and helps foster a healthier, more vibrant community and economy.

THE ESSENCE AND IMPACT OF CELEBRATION

Celebration is a universal human experience, marking significant moments and achievements with joy and festivity for individuals and communities. It transcends cultures, borders, and backgrounds, serving as a powerful tool for expression and connection. Whether it's a personal milestone like a birthday or a collective occasion like a national holiday, celebrations play a crucial role in shaping our lives and societies.

The Purpose of Celebration

At its core, celebration is about acknowledgment and appreciation. It allows us to pause and reflect on the achievements or events that matter to us, providing a sense of closure and fulfillment. Celebrations can range from intimate events, such as family dinners to honor graduation, to grandiose events, such as elaborate parades for cultural or religious festivals. Regardless of the scale, celebrating highlights the significance of moments and individuals, reinforcing bonds among participants and giving meaning to our routines.

Cultural and Social Dimension

Celebrations are deeply embedded in cultural identities and express a community's values, beliefs, and traditions. For instance, Diwali, the Hindu festival of lights, celebrates the triumph of good over evil with fireworks, sweets, and lighting lamps, reflecting the community's emphasis on hope and renewal. Similarly, Thanksgiving in the United States revolves around gratitude and brings families together to reflect on what they are thankful for, reinforcing familial and societal bonds.

Socially, celebrations promote inclusivity and learning. They open doors to the uninitiated, offering insights into different cultures and lifestyles through participatory experiences. For example, public celebrations like Carnival in Brazil or Mardi Gras in New Orleans provide entertainment and promote cultural understanding and tourism, showcasing local customs, music, and cuisine to the world.

Psychological Benefits

Celebrating also has significant psychological benefits. It generates positivity and excitement, fostering happiness and contentment. Engaging in festive activities can reduce stress and increase life satisfaction by providing breaks from the routine stresses of life. Moreover, celebrations connected with personal achievements, such as career promotions or completing a major project, boost self-esteem and motivate further personal and professional development.

Economic Impact

Beyond personal and cultural aspects, celebrations also have a tangible economic impact. Major festivals and public holidays can drive significant economic activity, from increased retail sales to tourism. Businesses often see a surge in sales around major holidays, and local economies benefit from festivals through job creation and increased spending on food, accommodations, and entertainment. This economic uplift can be essential for small communities, where annual festivals might attract visitors from around the globe.

§

In essence, celebrations are a vital part of human life. They enrich our experiences, enhance our well-being, and strengthen our connections with others. Through celebrations, we express joy, forge communal ties, and recognize the milestones that give life depth and flavor. By marking achievements and traditions with festivity, we honor the past and present and inspire hope and enthusiasm for the future. Celebrations remind us of the beauty of life and the importance of taking moments to revel in existence together simply.

SUMMING UP THIS BOOK

SHORT CUTS TO BEING THE DOMINANT PERSON IN YOUR INDUSTRY

1.) Experts write books. As a cosmetic surgeon, I wrote 17 books that established me as a leading cosmetic surgeon. Since I retired, I've written three international best-selling books

   A.) The Secrets to A Fantastic Life - co-authored with Harriet Tinka and with a forward by NYT best-selling author Jack Canfieldget your copy here www.drallenlycka.com

   B.) The Pillars of Success – Co-written with Jack Canfield - get your copy here www.drallenlycka.com

   C.) bLU volume 1 - Cowritten with Corey Poirier - get your copy here www.drallenlycka.com

2.) Experts win awards . As a cosmetic surgeon I received the Cosmetic Surgery Award for 16 consecutive years. This is why I created the IOFP. In its second year, I will be introducing a new award that all inductees will be eligible for

3.) Experts are acknowledged. That's why I'm creating networking events and galas where they can be acknowledged, communicate and collaborate with like-thinking top-tier professionals.

4.) Experts share their knowledge. That's why I am creating unique opportunities with books, magazine and podcast participation

5.) Experts give back and "pay it forward". That's why I'm "giving back" by creating scholarship programs

6.) Authorities have drive. I call it the "hunger". Every member has that drive. That's how they got to where they are. Sometimes this has to be rekindled and that is what associating with other experts does.

7.) Authorities have a clear message. The IOFP is the organization where quality matters and integrity counts.

8.) Authorities are seen with other authorities. As a celebrity, I had photos with:

- Jack Canfield

- Paula Abdul

- Dr. Oz

- Tony Robbins

- Brendon Burchard

- Others

9.) Experts speak on stages. As a cosmetic surgeon, I spoke on podiums with other greats around the world — from Ho Chi Min City to Sun City, South Africa, from Las Vegas to NYC, from Vancouver to LA. As a professional speaker, these are a few of the stages I've been on:

- AAD - multiple lectures 2003-2019

- AAD -2013-2017

- CSF - Las Vegas, Nashville December 2013-2017

- CSI- Dubaï 2016

- DASIL Ho ChiMinh City, 2017

- DASIL Sun City, South Africa 2017

- CSF - Nashville 2018

- Harvard University - Oct 2019

- TEDx Grande Prairie -2020

- University of Alberta - 2022

- UCLA - 2023

- Iowa Hospital Association Nov 2023
- National Management Week Sept 2023
- University of Calgary July 2023
- University of Alberta August 2023
- Anderson University Oct 2023
- Disrupt HR Las Vegas Sept 2023
- Disrupt HR Northern Colorado Oct 2023
- Disrupt HR Waterloo- Kitchner Oct 2023
- Disrupt HR San Antonio, Oct 2023
- Greenville, SC - Nov 2023
- TEDx U of A 2024
- Disrupt HR - Sioux Falls April 2024
- Disrupt HR Albuquerque April 2024
- Disrupt Austin May 2024
- Disrupt Las Angeles May 2024
- Disrupt Chicago May 2024
- Disrupt Halifax May 2024
- Disrupt Portland. ME June 2024
- PBS event — May 2024
- SHRM Sandusky, Ohio - Sept 2024
- SHRM Grand Forks, N.D.- Sept 2024
- SHRM Memphis Tennessee - Aug 2024
- SHRM Albuquerque April- 2024
- ProEd CMED's - Phoenix, Nov 2024
- NFDA New Orleans - Oct. 2024
- Tony Walker Financial - Bowling Green Kentucky, Oct 2024
- WFLA Spokane May 2024
- IAOTP Summer Soirée Toronto Ontario Canada July 2024

The IOFP gives unique opportunities to speak around the world. It enhances members' credibility and provides video and photographic proof of credibility.

10.) Experts have a great team. The IOFP shares its great team, helping you maintain your status as the leading expert in your area

11.) Experts engage in shameless self-promotion. This is something most people find distasteful. The IOFP allows you to promote without self-promotion.

12.) Experts give to get.

13.) I wrote about the Triangle of Pre-eminence™ in the early 2000s. It consists of three things - each point represented by the corner of a triangle:

   i.   Expertise and extraordinary customer service

   ii.   Extraordinary marketing

   iii. Customer service

This triad is the secret to dominate ANY market, and all 13 points allow you to develop expertise and stay there. The IOFP is there to help you and your IOFP is there to guide you along the way.

14.) Experts celebrate their success

15.) Experts live fantastic lives every day. They don't live to work, they work to live

The IOFP is dedicated to help our members establish themselves as the expert in their field through acknowledgement, communication and collaboration. It's a community where expertise matters and integrity counts.

Check us out at www.FantasticProfessionals.com and if you are interested call us at 844.936.3362 or write us at info@fantasticprofessionals.com or tami@fantasticprofessionals.com